Manischewitz: The Matzo Family

The Making of an American Jewish Icon

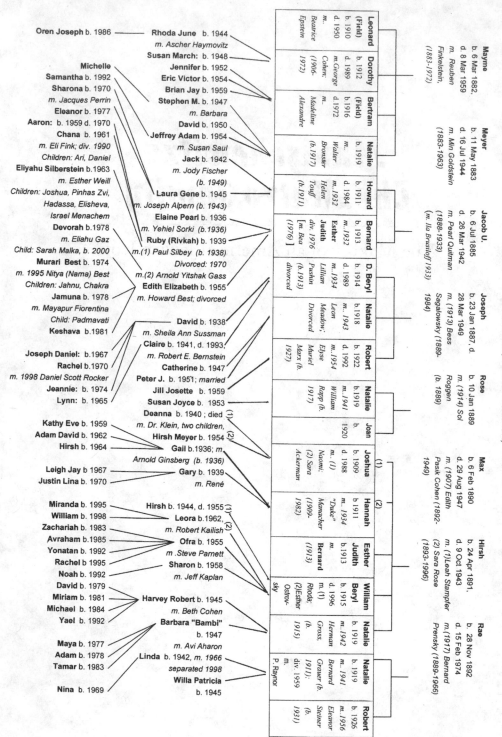

Dov Behr Manischewitz: b. 1857 d. 8 March 1914,
m. Nesha Rose (b. 1857- d. 17 June 1916)

Oren Joseph b. 1986 —— Rhoda June b. 1944
m. Ascher Haymovitz
Susan March: b. 1948

Leonard (Field) b. 1910 m. 1950 Beatrice Epstein

Mayne b. 6 Mar 1882, d. 8 Mar 1959 m. Reuben Finkelstein, (1883-1972)

Michelle
Samantha b. 1992
Sharona b. 1970
m. Jacques Perrin
Eleanor b. 1977
Aaron: b. 1959 d. 1970
Chana b. 1961
m. Eli Fink; div. 1990
Children: Ari, Daniel
Eliyahu Silberstein b.1963
m. Esther Weill
Children: Joshua, Pinhas Zvi,
Hadassa, Elisheva,
Israel Menachem
Devorah b.1978
m. Eliahu Gaz
Child: Sarah Malka, b. 2000
Murari Best b. 1974
m. 1995 Nitya (Nama) Best
Children: Jahnu, Chakra
Jamuna b. 1978
m. Mayapur Fiorentina
Child: Padmavati
Keshava b.1981

Jennifer b. 1952
Eric Victor b. 1954
Brian Jay b. 1959
Stephen M. b. 1947
m. Barbara
David b. 1950
Jeffrey Adam b. 1954
m. Susan Saul
Jack b. 1942
m. Jody Fischer
(b. 1949)
Laura Gene b. 1945
m. Joseph Alpern (b. 1943)
Elaine Pearl b. 1936
m. Yehiel Sorki (b.1936)
Ruby (Rivkah) b. 1939
m.(1) Paul Silbey (b. 1938)
Divorced: 1970
m.(2) Arnold Yitshak Gass
Edith Elizabeth b. 1955
m. Howard Best; divorced

Dorothy (Field) b. 1912 d. 1989 m. George Cohen; (1906-1972)

Meyer b. 11 May 1883 d. 16 Jul 1944 m. Min Goldstein (1883-1963)

Jacob U. b. 6 Jul 1885 d. 26 Mar 1942 m. Pearl Quitman (1888-1933) (m. Ila Brastloff 1933)

Bertram (Field) b. 1916 d. 1972 m. Madeline Alexandre

Natalie b. 1919 m. Walter Bronster (b.1917)

Howard b. 1911 d. 1984 m. Helen Toiff (b.1911)

Bernard b. 1913 m. 1932 Esther Pushin (b. 1913)

Joseph b. 23 Jan 1887. d. 28 Mar 1949 m. (1913) Bess Sagalowsky (1889- 1984)

David b. 1938
m. Sheila Ann Sussman
Claire b. 1941, d. 1993;
m. Robert E. Bernstein
Catherine b. 1947
Peter J. b. 1951; married
Jill Josette b. 1959
Susan Joyce b. 1953
Deanna b. 1940 ; died
m. Dr. Klein, two children,
Hirsh Meyer b. 1954
Gail b.1936; m.
Arnold Ginsberg (b. 1936)
Gary b. 1939
m. René

Joseph Daniel: b.1967
Rachel b.1970
m. 1998 Daniel Scott Rocker
Jeannie: b. 1974
Lynn: b. 1965

Kathy Eve b. 1959
Adam David b. 1962
Hirsh b. 1964

Leigh Jay b 1967
Justin Lina b. 1970

D. Beryl b. 1914 d. 1989 m. 1934 Lillian Pushin

Rose b. 10 Jan 1889 m. (1914) Sol Roggen (b. 1889)

Natalie b. 1918 m. 1943 Leon Meadow; Divorced

Robert b. 1922 d. 1992 m. 1954 Elyse Marx (b. 1927)

Natalie b. 1919 m.1941 William Rapp (b. 1917)

Max b. 6 Feb 1890 d. 29 Aug 1947 m. (1907) Edith Pasik Cohen (1892- 1949)

Joan b. 1920

Joshua b 1909 d. 1988 m. (1) Naomi; (2) Sara Ackerman

Hannah b 1911 m.1934 "Duke" Monacher (1909- 1982)

Miranda b. 1995
William b. 1998
Zachariah b. 1983
Avraham b.1985
Yonatan b. 1992
Rachel b 1995
Noah b. 1992
David b. 1979
Miriam b. 1981
Michael b. 1984
Yael b. 1992

Hirsh b. 1944, d. 1955
Leora b.1962,
m. Robert Kailish
Ofra b. 1955
m .Steve Parnett
Sharon b. 1958
m. Jeff Kaplan

Hirsh b. 24 Nov 1891, d. 9 Oct 1943 m. (1)Leah Stampler (2) Sara Rose Prensky (1893-1996)

Esther Judith (1913)

Maya b. 1977
Adam b. 1978
Tamar b. 1983

Nina b. 1969

Harvey Robert b. 1945
m. Beth Cohen
Barbara "Bambi" b. 1947
m. Avi Aharon
Linda b. 1942, m. 1966
separated 1998
Willa Patricia b. 1945

William Beryl b. 1915 d. 1996 m. (1) Rhoda; Ostrov- sky (2)Esther Gross, (b. 1915)

Natalie b. 1919 m.1942 Herman Grauer (b. 1911); div. 1959 m. P. Raynor

Rae b. 28 Nov 1892 d. 15 Feb 1974 m.(1917) Bernard Prensky (1889-1966)

Bernard b. 1913 d. 1996 m. (1) Bernard Steiner (b. 1931)

Robert b. 1926 m.1956 Eleanor Steiner (b. 1931)

Manischewitz: The Matzo Family

The Making of an American Jewish Icon

by

Laura Manischewitz Alpern

Introduction by

Jonathan D. Sarna
Joseph H. & Belle R. Braun Professor of American Jewish History
Brandeis University

KTAV Publishing House, Inc.
in Association with The American Jewish Historical Society

Library of Congress Cataloging-in-Publication Data

Alpern, Laura Manischewitz.
  Manischewitz, the matzo family : the making of an American Jewish icon / by Laura
Manischewitz Alpern.
    p. cm.
  ISBN 978-1-60280-003-8
  1. Manischewitz family. 2. Jews—Ohio—Cincinnati—History. 3. B. Manischewitz Co.
4. Jewish businesspeople—Ohio—Cincinnati—Biography. 5. Businesspeople—Ohio—
Cincinnati—Biography. 6. Matzos industry—Ohio—Cincinnati—History. 7. Cincinnati
(Ohio)—History. I. Title.
  F499.C59J524 2008
  977.1'7800492400922—dc22

Published by
KTAV Publishing House, Inc.
930 Newark Avenue
Jersey City, NJ 07306
Email: bernie@ktav.com
www.ktav.com
(201) 963-9524
Fax (201) 963-0102

Dedicated to the memory of my parents

Helen and Howard Manischewitz

Contents

Introduction

Twenty years ago, a member of the Manischewitz family, in Cincinnati for a private visit, turned up for services on Saturday morning at the synagogue where I was a member. He was treated like royalty.

"Manischewitz has returned," one old-timer exclaimed. Another recounted stories of the great matzo family, how it grew, and what the Manischewitz company had meant to Cincinnati Jews. Manischewitz received a prime honor during the service, and was mobbed by well-wishers the minute the service concluded. He seemed quite used to all the attention.

A few years later, in 1990, the eponymous company passed out of family control. Bernard Manischewitz sold it for $42.5 million to Kohlberg & Co. Since then, the firm, which now markets a wide variety of other kosher products, including matzo sold under the name of former competitors Horowitz-Margareten and Goodman's, has been sold two more times. In 1998 Millbrook Distribution Services, a subsidiary of R.A.B. Enterprises bought the company for $124.7 million. In turn R.A.B. sold the company in 2007 to Harbinger Capital Partners. Nevertheless, the name Manischewitz remains magical, an American Jewish icon.

Manischewitz is actually much more than just a name. It has become, through the years, a familiar symbol as well. For some it denotes Passover, the holiday when more people consume Manischewitz matzo than any other matzo in the world. For others, it represents kosher wine, the world's bestselling kosher wine, and the only one with a slogan ("Man, oh Manischewitz") that an astronaut, Gene Cernan, once actually exclaimed during a moonwalk. For still others, it epitomizes *everything* that makes food kosher. "Represent yourself as being a 100% Kosher individual with this, our newest Manischewitz shirt," an on-line magazine named *Jewcy* exclaims. Its hip Manischewitz® kosher shirts speak volumes concerning the Matzo Family's enduring legacy.

The B. Manischewitz Company began 120 years ago when its founder, Dov Behr, born in Salant, Lithuania, immigrated to Cincinnati in 1886 from the port city of Memel, then under Prussian rule. For a time, the newcomer peddled and slaughtered kosher meat in the city. Having slaughtered meat under the supervision of the famed Rabbi Israel Salanter, he was held in high regard. But in 1888, the enterprising immigrant branched out into matzo-baking. This was a common profession for Jewish immigrants, especially those trained in ritual slaughtering, for matzo too was a Jewish food strictly regulated by Jewish law and requiring supervision. Moreover, demand for matzo was rising steadily in the United States, keeping pace with the growth of America's Jewish population.

At the time that Manischewitz entered the matzo business, the industry was in a state of flux. For millennia, matzo had been made totally by hand. Then, in 1838, an Alsatian Jew named Isaac Singer, influenced by the industrial revolution, produced the first known machine for rolling matzo dough. The machine changed and shortened the process of matzo baking, increased the available supply, and led to a concomitant reduction in its price.

Beginning in 1859, the matzo machine became embroiled in a sharp and very significant religious controversy. A distinguished rabbi named Solomon Kluger published a learned manifesto declaring machine-made matzo to be a violation of Jewish law. Another distinguished rabbi named Joseph Saul Nathanson (who happened to be Rabbi Kluger's brother-in-law) totally disagreed and published an equally learned manifesto in defense of machine-made matzo. The subsequent arguments back and forth embroiled rabbis around the world. Could the matzo machine fulfill the requirement of *kavannah* (intentionality) in baking matzo? Was it fully reliable in preventing leaven from entering the process? Should Jewish communities maintain expensive hand-made traditions of baking matzo to provide work for poor people, or was it better to encourage cheaper machine-made matzo that even poor people could afford?

Finally, and one suspects most importantly, the matzo machine kindled arguments concerning modernity. Supporters promoted the idea that modern technology could strengthen traditional Judaism; indeed, some rabbis optimistically argued that technology could produce better and more kosher matzos than Jews had ever enjoyed before. Meanwhile, opponents feared that machine-made matzo, like so many other innovations in matters of religious tradition, would become a dangerous instrument of modernity leading inevitably to assimilation, Reform, and apostasy. These vituperative arguments were by no means settled by the time Manischewitz became involved in the matzo business. To the contrary, the Jewish world of his day was divided between those who accepted matzo made with the assistance of a machine and those who did not.

In rapidly industrializing America, where the Jewish population was multiplying and demand for matzo grew year by year, machine-made matzo found increasing support. A primitive matzo machine was described in New York Jewish newspapers as early as 1850. Behr Manischewitz, a born tinkerer, would greatly improve on the technology for baking matzo. He and his gifted son, Jacob Uriah (Jake), who succeeded him upon his untimely death in 1914, created machines that automated the entire process of matzo making. By the 1920s, Manischewitz could boast of being the world's largest manufacturers of matzo, producing some 1.25 million matzos per day. Their factory in 1938 housed "the largest and most expensive single piece of machinery in any bakery in the world."

A study of "ethnic foods and the making of Americans," by Donna R. Gabaccia, argues that food customs tied to religious beliefs "encouraged a particularly intense culinary conservatism" among immigrant groups like the Jews. Matzo, the quintessential Passover religious food seems at first glance, to exemplify this pattern. Indeed, Behr Manischewitz adhered scrupulously to Jewish law in all aspects of matzo baking. For years, his company advertised that its matzos were the "most kosher matzos in the world."

Yet for all of its outward conservatism, Manischewitz was really a revolutionary force in the long history of matzo. In addition to converting millions of Jews to machine-made matzo, it also transformed the product itself in three major ways. First, where before most matzo had been round, irregular or oval-shaped, now, largely because of the demands of technology and packaging, it became square. Second, where before each matzo was unique and distinctive in terms of shape, texture, and overall appearance, now, every matzo in the box came out looking, feeling, and tasting the same. Manischewitz matzo thus became a distinctive *brand* of matzo, with all that that implied. Third, where before matzo was a quintessentially local product, produced on an as-needed basis in every Jewish community and not shipped vast distances for fear of breakage, now it became a national product and then an international one.

Remarkably, Manischewitz staged this revolution without calling down upon itself the jackals of heresy. The scrupulous reputation for piety of Behr Manischewitz and also of his son, Hirsch, who spent thirteen years studying in various yeshivot (Talmudical academies) in Jerusalem, helped the company to win significant rabbinic allies. The generosity of the Manischewitz family to Orthodox causes in the United States and Palestine proved important as well. Though many Hasidic and other East European rabbis continued to oppose machine-made matzo on principle, no fewer than 124 "leading figures of the generation," cited in 1938, including some of the most famous rabbis in the world such as Rabbi Abraham I. Kook of Jerusalem and Rabbi Meir Shapiro of

Lublin, attested to Manischewitz matzo's high standards of reliability. Decade after decade, Manischewitz, working within the confines of Jewish law, managed to synthesize the requirements of the Jewish faith with the most modern of contemporary technologies to produce more matzo for more people than any company in Jewish history.

Like so many ethnic food businesses, Manischewitz was primarily a family business. It passed from fathers to sons, and in some capacity or other employed a wide variety of family members. Laura Manischewitz Alpern, herself a scion of the family, reminds us in this book that families, especially large families like Manischewitz, are complicated and colorful. The women of the Manischewitz family—who, as in so many other cases, mostly operated behind the scenes—played an especially critical role. They might have played an even more critical business role, Alpern observes, had they but been given the chance. As for the men, they covered a broad spectrum: some more able than others, some more affable then others, some more religious than others. What united them, men and women alike, were bonds of kinship, as well as a firm allegiance to the Jewish people.

Through the years the Manischewitz family built on its ties to the Jewish people. Theirs was what would today be called a "niche market"—Jewish food—and it was a market that family members understood intuitively. Seeking, like all successful ethnic merchants, to broaden their base, the Manischewitzes eventually expanded both horizontally and vertically. They moved from Cincinnati to the center of Jewish life in New York. They exported matzo to Jewish communities around the world, including Russia and the Land of Israel. And they branched out from matzo, a food mostly consumed during Passover, to year-round products like Tam Tam crackers, gefilte fish, and especially kosher wine (which was actually produced by an outside company under license.) As the twentieth century wound down, Manischewitz was, by far, America's best known and largest producer of kosher foods. It had become the quintessential kosher food brand.

By then, perhaps inevitably, the business had outgrown the family that created it. Bernard Manischewitz, in 1990, found no obvious successor to himself among family members, and put the company up for sale. Many other ethnic food companies had shifted from family control to corporate control through the years: Ronzoni, Franco-American, La Choy, Lender's and innumerable others. Ethnic foods were becoming American foods, their distinctive origins forgotten.

Thanks to Laura Manischewitz Alpern, the origins of Manischewitz will not be forgotten. She recounts the family's history through the lives of its leading men and women. Her insider's tale of the family that transformed the world of matzo and became a symbol of "100% kosher" reminds us why the name "Manischewitz" remains magical still. Man, oh Manischewitz, what a story!

Jonathan D. Sarna
Joseph H. & Belle R. Braun Professor of American Jewish History
Brandeis University

Chapter 1

Out of Egypt

*We were slaves to Pharaoh in Egypt, and the Lord our
God took us out from there with a strong hand and with
an outstretched arm. If the Holy One, blessed be He, had
not taken our fathers out of Egypt, then we, our children,
and our children's children would have remained en-
slaved to Pharaoh in Egypt.*

—Passover Haggadah

There were moments in Nesha's childhood that would stay with
her all her life. Standing in the doorway on a chilly school morning with a stiff Baltic wind blowing in from the port was one of
these moments. The mornings were all the same. "Keep away
from the port," Nesha's mother warned, an anxious frown on the
bit of forehead that poked out under her heavy wool head-cov-
ering. Sturdy, round-faced Nesha scrutinized her mother patiently
as the words washed over her. Perhaps the reason the moment
stayed in her mind was that a few years later her life would be focused precisely on that forbidden port. Then the childhood
mornings would come back to her. She would picture before her
the tired woman who was her mother: a shapeless housewife in a
faded dress, with a limited repertoire of constantly repeated mo-
tions, words, and gestures. In her memory, Nesha herself was always about nine years old and wrapped in layers of well-worn
clothing, looking as if she could hardly move at all, let alone run
off to the port.

Keep away from the port.

In fact this was a literal impossibility. The port pierced its way through the heart of the city of Memel, today known as Klaipeda. Over the rooftops of the narrow houses, the masts of seagoing ships could be seen wobbling crazily in the wind.

Nesha's best friend, Feigel, waited nearby, as she did every morning, likewise bundled up against the gusty wind that blew wisps of hair across her thin face. Feigel rolled her eyes comically. Both girls both found it hilarious that Nesha's mother repeated the same warning every single morning. Of course, there was only one possible answer.

"Yes, Mama. Goodbye, Mama."

Within moments the two girls were as free as the wind, holding hands and running down the narrow street in the direction of school. Today, exceptionally, Nesha had been given a penny and the right to stop at the bakery.

Pink-cheeked and breathless, the girls entered the little bakery. In a moment the transaction was done and a warm roll was in Nesha's hand, to be shared with her friend.

"You girls should be grateful to Rabbi Ruelf that you're allowed to attend school," said the baker's wife, in a doubtful tone that left the girls free to guess whether she herself approved of so much liberty for young girls.

The girls nodded shyly and turned to leave. As soon as they were out of the bakery they were overcome by giggling. "Thank you, Rabbi Ruelf," said Nesha, waving her arms skywards in a forbidden priestly blessing. She'd peeked at the men in the synagogue, so she knew how this was done.

What the baker's wife said was true enough. Nesha and her friend were born in 1857, a good year for the growing Jewish community of Memel. Nine girls and seven boys were born that year, bringing their numbers just over eight hundred. Rabbi Yitzhak Ruelf had arrived a few years earlier to serve as rabbi of the German Jewish community. He was a devout man, but even so, he approved of Jewish boys and girls attending public schools.

His word carried a lot of weight, even among pious East European Jews like Nesha's parents.

The half-day spent at school was the girls' unique escape from the narrow streets they lived on and the narrow lives they were destined for. They loved it.

This morning, like every morning, Nesha and Feigel approached the tall public school building hand in hand and entered through the creaking wooden door grayed by decades of salt spray. They found their seats on a bench in an unheated classroom and waited contentedly for the day to begin. Nesha and her best friend were not troublesome children. Giggling at the slightest provocation was probably their worst sin.

The entire class rose in unison when their teacher entered the room. Then, with a noisy creaking of benches, they settled into place, looking like so many potatoes, bundled up in coats and scarves in the barely heated building.

"We will be having a geology lesson this morning," said the teacher, a thin, nervous man with a bookish voice. Nesha listened expectantly. It hardly mattered which lesson it was. It was all material for her dreams.

"You see here some examples of amber. Amber is not a stone. It is the fossilized resin of trees that were buried in this region thousands of years ago. These pieces of amber were found on the beach at a resort named Polangen, located thirty miles north of here." He paused to look at his blank-faced charges. Thirty miles up the coast, or thirty thousand—it was all the same to them, beyond the edges of their world. Perhaps sensing this, he made the children rise and troop past his lectern so that each in turn could observe the bright orange substance.

When her turn came, Nesha looked as long as she dared. A fly was trapped in one of the amber blocks. She imagined it breaking loose and landing softly on her forehead. As she walked slowly back to her seat, she let her mind wander up and down the sandy beach at the place with such a tantalizing name. When they were both seated, she nudged Feigel and whispered, "One day I'll ride in a carriage to Polangen. I'll go to the beach and gather up a whole bucket full of amber."

"No you won't," whispered Feigel. "Will," hissed Nesha, knowing very well that she would not. Her whole life was traced out for her, like the neat lines she traced in her copybook. *Here you can walk*, she said to herself, and drew a firm black line in the copybook, *and there you can't. You can walk on this street, but not that one. You can obey your mother. You can't do schoolwork on the Sabbath. You can wear thick, ugly stockings. You can walk to the Friedrich's market IF you are accompanied.* A caged bird was freer than Nesha, for the cage door might one day be opened and the bird would escape, whereas Nesha was surrounded by cages within cages. And what if she strayed? A neighbor or relative would bring her home again.

And the restrictions would be unending. Marriage—far from the child's thoughts as she sat in the schoolroom—would be to a man not of her own choosing, and would carry an equal, though different, burden of limitations. Restrictions formed a web that made the young girl's life narrow, but also kept her safe in an uncertain world.

The forbidden port, for instance. Why would she ever want to wander there? Rough seamen and longshoremen were always hanging around all year long, for it never froze over. Ships were loaded or unloaded at all hours of the day or night. There were ugly-looking taverns near the port. Memel was a rough city, not a place where a little girl could play in a park or go for a walk on a tree-lined avenue with her parents—even if her parents would have done such a thing, which they would not. The town center was composed of grim, chunky buildings, all crowded around the port. There had been some attractive buildings with carved and painted wooden fronts, but children in Nesha's age group never saw them: most of them burned down or were damaged in the big fire of 1854. The hastily rebuilt sections of town were even uglier than the rest. So that there was nowhere of interest to go, even if she were free to wander.

While Nesha dreamed of beaches strewn with amber, the geology lesson ended and was followed by geography. Names like London, Paris, Vienna lit up the frayed map pinned onto the wall. A girl could dream of all these places. And better yet—though it was not on the map—she could dream of America. The teacher said little of real interest about America. Much of his discourse concerned industry or the history of wars and settlements. But a girl could imagine. Nesha imagined herself going to the port, not on foot but in a shiny black carriage, with a ticket and a suitcase and a fur hat, and getting on a ship headed for America.

"That's all for today," the teacher said, glancing up at the tall window where the pale northern sun had dipped very slightly past its peak, only to be promptly concealed behind a neighboring building.

At those words the boys in the class jumped up from their seats like soldiers released from captivity in an enemy camp. Nesha and Feigel rose unwillingly. The end of the short school day meant their return to apartments scarcely warmer than the school building, where each girl was obliged to help her mother in an endless round of housework.

Holidays were worse, especially the Gentile holidays, which for Nesha meant an entire day of housework interrupted only by errands for her mother to shops on the nearby streets. Any schoolwork had to be done in snatched moments between tasks. A girl's schooling was not important enough to take priority over helping her mother.

On Jewish holidays, the restrictions on Nesha's activities were even greater. There were restrictions concerning the preparation of the holiday meals (all cooking had to be done in advance of the Sabbath, while on other holidays cooking could be done, but only in a particular way). There were restrictions on how the cleaning up could be done (with cold water only). And there were restrictions on what she could do when her work was finished: for instance, such activities as writing, drawing, and knitting were forbidden on the Sabbath.

Yet there was a sweetness about the Sabbath, when all the everyday objects were laid aside and forgotten. Listening to her father chanting the Sabbath prayers gave her a peaceful, holy feeling. Nesha never doubted that God was protecting the little world she lived in. She often thought that God was right in the room, perhaps above the Sabbath candles listening to her father saying the prayers. The menacing sounds in the distance—the shouts of sailors and the thudding sounds of ships taking on cargo—seemed to be held at bay by the quiet, holy words said over the lovingly set Sabbath table.

Holidays or schooldays, Nesha dressed meticulously whenever she went out. She began to do this from the time she was a girl of nine or ten. She wore the plain long sleeves, long skirt, and thick stockings that her pious upbringing required of her. But it would seem that looking her best springs straight from a girl's heart, not from her upbringing.

For she always managed to look good. Every day she brushed her thick, wavy brown hair till it was glossy and smooth. She pinched her round cheeks to make them pink, and noted with satisfaction how this made her big blue eyes look even bluer.

"You always look so pretty," Feigel said, when they met for their morning walk to school. Nesha loved to see the frank admiration in her friend's eyes, and the way housewives in their doorways nodded at her in approval.

It wasn't the same as being allowed to come and go as she pleased. But it gave her some measure of control over her life, and this was enough to quench her restlessness. In some dark corner of her mind, she knew that she needed something more—but what? She knew no words for it.

* * *

Toward the end of the 1860s, when Nesha finished school, Memel was beginning its slow decline. The annual fairs, which had attracted as many as fifteen thousand Jewish merchants and nearly as many Gentile ones, were beginning to lose their importance. Nesha and her girlfriends found the fairs boring anyway. They were mostly devoted to trade in timber and flax, and offered very little of interest to young girls.

As new railroad lines were built, the role of the fairs would diminish further. Instead of growing and flourishing, the port city of Memel would gradually stagnate, then fall victim to wars and conquests, and finally sink into bleak anonymity.

A dismal future awaited the Jews of Memel. The next expulsion of Jews was just around the corner, in the mid-eighties. All Jews who did not have Prussian citizenship—and they were the majority—would be menaced with expulsion, and only Rabbi Ruelf's energetic intervention would result in a compromise that allowed many to remain.

The Jews would be menaced once again in 1914, on the eve of the First World War, and would live a tenuous existence until one day in 1939 when it would all end in flames on *Kristalnacht*. The synagogues would be destroyed. The Jews would flee to the surrounding Lithuanian towns, where death soon would find them at the hands of the Nazi murderers and their local henchmen.

But the situation of the city was only of marginal interest to Nesha, who had more important things to think of. From the day she finished school, her life revolved around one thing: making herself ready for the marriage that would one day be arranged for her. As she grew older—eighteen, nineteen, and then entering her twenties—she focused all her attention on this. The vague restlessness of her childhood was gone. Now she wanted the best for herself. Inevitably, "the best" meant only one thing: the best bridegroom. A young woman could refuse a bridegroom. This right was guaranteed by Jewish law. But why would she want to? She couldn't refuse to live in the world. And in this world, any other alternatives were surely a lot worse than accepting the bridegroom proposed to her.

Her papa's status in the pious community was what counted most in making a match. Luckily her papa was known for his piety, though he wasn't a scholar or well off. This was a reason for optimism. But Nesha was not a girl to leave everything to fate. She made sure that she was seen daily as she went about her real or imaginary errands, greeting the neighbor women politely with a smile, and lowering her eyes demurely before the men. Young men usually managed to find out about a girl's looks and reputation, even though they were kept at a distance.

Her schooling was a definite asset in the marriage market. Nesha could read German, and the Hebrew prayers too, but Yiddish was the language she knew best. She liked the sound of the Hebrew prayers and the feeling of piety it gave her when she could read them correctly. *See what a pious girl I am*, she told an imaginary matchmaker as she bent over her prayer book, at the same time hoping it was not impious to think such proud thoughts. *Can't you see I'll be a perfect bride for a pious man, for a scholar?*

* * *

While Nesha spent her days running errands and peeling potatoes and doing the laundry and learning to prepare a chicken for the Sabbath meal, her future bridegroom was bent over his holy books, learning page after page of Talmud by heart. His name was Dov Behr, son of Yehiel Michael, and he was a student at a renowned school of Jewish learning, the Telshe yeshiva, located in the town called Telz in Yiddish and Telšiai in Lithuanian.

Dov Behr didn't have time for daydreaming. The school day at Telz was physically and mentally exhausting: the students recited their prayers at eight, then went back to their rooms for breakfast. They had their morning studies from ten till two-thirty, then there was a break for them to go to their lunch assignments at the homes of members of the community. The meal they were given was often meager. *Essen teig*—"eating days"—was the name given to this arrangement in Yiddish.

The yeshiva in Telz (photographed in 1999)

Behr (he eventually left off the "Dov" except for formal occasions) had an older brother who had remained in Telz after completing his religious studies and married a local girl whom he met through a meal assignment. This was a big advantage for Behr. He took his midday meal at his brother's home instead of going to strangers. Not that the food was any better—his brother did a meager trade in grain, and his sister-in-law kept a small cafe in the town, and together they just barely managed to scrape by. But it was agreeable to have the midday respite from the communal life of the yeshiva.

At four-thirty the boys all went back to the yeshiva and studied together until nine-thirty at night. After that they had another half hour of lighter study, for which they were allowed to make their own choice of books. At ten they said their evening prayers and went home to eat a light meal and sleep. The best students, though, would go back to the yeshiva and stay up till midnight, studying. Behr was usually among them.

Harsh as the conditions were, it was a privilege to study at the famous school. Boys came from as far away as Poland and the southern German principalities to study there.

Behr himself had not traveled so far. His home was in the Lithuanian village of Salantai, known to Jews as Salant, some seventy miles from Memel. It was a relatively well-off village, on a main trade route. About nine hundred Jews lived there, nearly as many as lived in Memel. His father made a decent living by combining a job teaching Hebrew to young boys at the local *cheder* with a little commerce in grain and flax. But still, it was just a village. Behr had no intention of returning to live in his village.

Memel was the destination he had in mind as he neared the end of his studies. Memel and its port.

* * *

Meanwhile, Nesha had reached the advanced age of twenty-two, still single. Most of her old classmates were already married, except for her faithful friend Feigel. In Nesha's rear courtyard, the two friends sat on the flat washing stone and reviewed the facts of their situation from every possible angle. Their discussion had all the seriousness of a town council meeting.

"First of all," Nesha said to Feigel, "we mustn't forget that each of us has our destined bridegroom, our *beschert*."

Feigel nodded. "Marriages are in God's hands." Her voice wavered. "So we shouldn't be worried." "Right."

"But our fathers have to find him," Feigel said. "And when your father went to Telz on business last year, and got sick there and stayed until he was, thank God, well again, he couldn't think about a match for you."

Nesha nodded; that had been a definite setback.

"And then your sister still had to be married."

"Of course, right. Papa couldn't begin to think of a match for me before my sister was married!"

This was the unwritten law.

"At least she's married now, thank God!"

Nesha thought very briefly of her older sister—once an obstacle, now happily removed.

"So it will soon be your turn, Nesha." Feigel sighed as she said this. Her own older sister had a limp and was not yet married. She would have to wait even longer.

A few long months went by.

One Sabbath morning Nesha felt a sort of electricity in the air. It began at home as she dressed, and it pursued her down the street and into the synagogue, where she found her girlfriends clustered together upstairs in the women's section of the synagogue.

Nesha and her unmarried friends always attended Sabbath prayer services at the big synagogue rather than the small neighborhood synagogue. Upstairs in the women's balcony, they could sit and gossip freely. Attendance at the Sabbath morning prayer service was not required for married women with family responsibilities.

As soon as Nesha arrived, Feigel grasped her arm and whispered to her excitedly.

"Your father has found a bridegroom for you, I can tell."

"How can you tell?" Nesha whispered back. Two or three other girls leaned closer to listen.

"I saw your papa talking before the service with my uncle and with Rabbi Salanter, and the three of them never usually talk together, and I heard my uncle tell my papa there is a new young man from Salant here."

Nesha's face flushed. "Well, we will soon know if you are right, won't we?" she said in a voice that shook just a little.

"Won't we now!" Feigel herself looked as excited as Nesha, for she was a true friend. One or two of the other young women looked frankly envious.

They peered down at the busy scene below. On the main floor of the synagogue, men were shuffling around, some gesticulating as if in conversation, others already wrapped in their shawls, deep in prayer. Boys of all sizes fidgeted or imitated their fathers, swaying in prayer.

Nesha easily spotted the silvery haired figure of Rabbi Yisroel Salanter in the crowd below her.

The distinguished rabbi was an old man of nearly seventy, an amazing person, much admired by her father and the other men of the congregation, still remembered in history as the founder of the Musar movement. He was a brilliant scholar and had been in Memel ever since she was a small child. Rabbi Salanter did not lead a congregation. He had never wanted to do this, even though he could easily have become the rabbi of another town. The men in Memel studied with him whenever they had the opportunity.

Nesha used to think the men only spoke of holy subjects with the rabbi. Was it possible that today they had actually been talking about her, Nesha?

She had to wait for the day to pass. After lunch, her father would spend long hours at the house of study with the other men. After that he would return to the synagogue, and remain there until darkness announced the end of the Sabbath.

Finally it was evening. Nesha's father returned home, where his daughter awaited him. He carefully removed his coat and placed it on a hook. He performed the ceremony marking the end of the Sabbath, using the ritual items— twisted candle, spices, and wine—that Nesha's mother had laid out for him. Then he said the magic words:

"I have found a groom for you, Nesha. A new arrival in Memel, a serious, religious, hard-working, and ambitious young man, originally from Salant, and highly recommended by Rabbi Salanter, may he live for long years."

"Yes, Papa." So it was true! Nesha luxuriated in the wave of delight that washed over her.

"The young man's name is Dov Behr son of Yehiel Michael," he continued. "A scholar, may his light shine in Israel. He has completed his studies in Telz. A fine young man of twenty-three years, your own age, my daughter."

Nesha did not even try to speak.

Her father waited a moment before adding, almost as an afterthought, "And so my daughter is pleased?"

It was not really a question. She didn't need to be pleased, if it came to that. And of course she was pleased. Her face was glowing with pleasure.

"Yes, Papa," she managed to say at last.

Her father went on to say that he hoped she would be deserving of such a fine young man. That she had been raised to be a modest young woman, and he would be proud to see her become a virtuous wife and, God willing, a mother of pious sons, and so on.

Nesha did not need to be told once again about being a virtuous wife. Her whole education at home had prepared her for it.

Her thoughts were on a new idea that had entered her mind. It had to do with just one word in Papa's description of her future husband: *ambitious*. Lately the word seemed to be in everyone's mouth. And in conversations, it was always coupled with another word—America. "My apprentice is ambitious," the baker's wife had said last week, nodding toward the boy sweeping the floor. "He'll go to America and become rich some day." America! Would that be her destiny?

From within her reverie, she noticed her father looking at her expectantly. "I'll do my best, Father, God willing." These seemed to be the right words, for he smiled benevolently and nodded to her, signifying that the conversation was over.

She turned to leave the room, glad to be alone with all the new thoughts that were tumbling about in her mind.

America. She was ready for it. She was ready for her ambitious bridegroom to carry her off to America. Some girls were so attached to their childhood home and family that they wept at their own weddings. Not Nesha! She wouldn't weep at leaving home. She was already infatuated with the man she had not yet met— a shadowy figure made up of little more than a black coat, a hat, and a broad forehead with "ambition" written on it.

What else did she know about him? He must be very bright as well as pious, for only a gifted boy would be sent all the way from his village to Telz to study. And next, why had he come here from Telz? There were plenty of pious families in Telz, so he could easily have found a bride there. But he'd left Telz and come to Memel. Why? Sometimes young men came to Memel to avoid military service. Jewish boys had to serve for an unbelievable period of twenty years in the tsar's army if they were drafted. But Behr was old enough to be safe from military conscription. Which left only one possibility, the one she'd thought of first of all: *he had come to Memel because he was planning to emigrate to America.*

All week long she hummed as she mended pillowcases and hemmed sheets and put together a pile of things to bring with her to the tiny apartment she would share with her husband. In order to learn about married life, she and her friend Feigel made a Sabbath afternoon visit to the home of a married girlfriend named Shayna.

Sabbath afternoon was a deliciously quiet time, the only time in the week when there was no real work to be done in the young wife's household, except for tending the baby and straightening up the kitchen. The scrubbing of pots and other major cleanup would be left till after nightfall, when the Sabbath was over.

Nesha and Feigel knocked softly on the door of the apartment, in case the baby was sleeping.

They were ushered in quietly to drink tea and sit with Shayna in her kitchen. There they could talk in low voices for hours, until dusk signaled the young husband's imminent return from the synagogue.

"Tell us about married life," Nesha said.

Feigel giggled. "Tell Nesha how she must always obey her husband," she said. Shayna thought for a moment. "You know," she said, "the law says a woman must always obey her husband. It's true, but in another way it isn't."

Nesha objected.

"A woman always has to go where her husband wants to go. If he wants to go to America, and she doesn't, she still must do it."

"That's a perfect example!" Shayna raised her voice, then lowered it again. "Of how a woman can have her way."

Her little audience leaned closer.

"Look at Appleman the butcher. He talked about emigrating, but his wife, Leah, always found a reason why they couldn't go *just yet.*"

The two listeners nodded.

"Well, in fact," Shayna said, "the woman did more than that. She encouraged her husband to become close to his father. Now her husband cherishes the old man, may he live to a hundred and twenty!" Shayna paused for effect, then continued. "Plus, the children adore their grandfather. She made sure of it. Could Appleman break his father's heart by leaving and taking the grandchildren from him?"

Shayna leaned back in her chair and folded her arms.

Nesha and Feigel looked at each other doubtfully.

"Well, that may be so," Nesha conceded. "But if your husband ever asks you to go to America, I hope you just say yes, and quickly! Unless you think that Memel is a fine place to live!" She must have spoken too loudly, for the baby awakened and the confidential talk was ended for the day.

* * *

Behr knew little more than his betrothed about America. Information was not easy to come by, and anyway he had been busy studying his holy books. But he knew that he wanted to be there, to be where the world was new and there was everything to discover. It was a dream that went back to his childhood in Salant.

Behr had spent his childhood with his parents in a comfortable village house that was painted bright green and had a smooth wooden floor and solidly thatched roof. The house was on a side street, nicely situated right near the synagogue. The synagogue itself stood at one end of the broad main street of the village, as far as possible from the ominously large stone Catholic church with gothic steeples, which stood facing off to it from a distance at the other end of the street, like a Goliath facing David.

Since their house was near the synagogue, it was convenient for the rabbi to come and visit. Behr's father was a good friend of the rabbi of Salant, who in fact spent much of his time in Memel, where he was known as "the Salanter rabbi," which meant "the rabbi from Salant," or sometimes as "Rabbi Salanter." When Behr was a boy, the rabbi often came to the house to visit his father, bringing with him a letter from some Salanter Jews— that was how he referred to Jews from Salant in America.

Usually the letter was from Cincinnati, where a whole community of Salanter Jews had settled. Often the letter included a request for advice from the rabbi on some weighty question where the opinions of the transplanted Salanter community were divided.

"Reb Yehiel," the rabbi would say— that was how he addressed Behr's father—"we have some serious matters before us." Then the rabbi would discuss the issue at length with Behr's father before replying to the letter. Listening to the talk of America, and the half-understood "serious matters" that generated such respect from his elders, Behr felt a chord of response, a desire to follow these strangers from his own village who had crossed the ocean and wrote such weighty letters from so far away. By the time he had first known his way around the village it had already been too small for him.

Behr told his father about his plan on the evening following his Bar Mitzvah, after a splendid performance in the synagogue.

"I aim to emigrate to America one day," he declared, clearing his throat self-consciously.

Instantly he felt a shift in his status with his father and the world. Behr's father had been strict with his son until the eve of this very day. He had corrected him many times with harsh physical punishment that seemed to mirror God's righteous anger at the Israelites in the Bible, so that the boy wholly accepted the rightness of it, and aimed to become as learned as his father, and equally fearsome in the eyes of his own future sons.

But this evening, when the boy announced his America plan, his father listened with respect. A son who was already showing brilliance in the study of Talmud was someone to reckon with. "Well, your education has only begun," said the father, in a voice that was almost man-to-man, "such a waste it would be to end it now. You must stay in Telz until you have become a scholar. Then, God willing, you may go to America."

Behr nodded. In fact he had no expectation of leaving immediately; only an orphan or an unschooled son of a desperately poor family would get on a boat alone at age thirteen. In America, there might be no Talmud scholars for him to learn from, and no wise men like his rabbi, to admire and imitate. He plunged into his studies with all his heart, and became a scholar. And now he was to get his reward: a good marriage and a good job in Memel.

Step one on the road to America.

Nesha was a little ashamed to realize where her thoughts were leading her. *I should be thinking of how to be a pious wife, not of frivolous things.* But the idea of America and the rumors of wealth there were all she could concentrate on. She took out her prayer book and forced herself to read straight through "A Woman of Valor" three times. But it was no use. What she wanted was to be was a woman of wealth. She wanted to be like the women in black silk dresses who traveled in shiny black carriages to the spa at Polangen.

The marriage of Nesha Rose of Memel and Dov Behr son of Yehiel Michael of Salant took place in the spring of 1881. The happy couple had only managed to glimpse each other briefly in the weeks before the wedding. It did not matter. Behr knew what he wanted and what the rabbi had promised him—a fine girl from a pious family. He had a quick look at her pink cheeks, her shy smile, and the rounded form that hinted at fertility. And Nesha was a contented bride. Nothing fazed her, not even her mother's stammered advice about how to bear up on the wedding night. *He will take me to America*, she thought for the hundredth time, right under the marriage canopy. She sipped the wine shyly from under her half-lifted veil. *I'll be a proud mother, I'll have little scholars for sons.* Her husband stomped on the glass, marking the official end of the ceremony. Nesha dreamed on. *In America I'll dress my daughters in frilly white dresses.* Friends and family called out a chorus of "mazal tov, mazal tov!" pulling her back to the present.

She beamed proudly as she was swept away with the women to one side, while her husband's arm was taken from the other side and he was led into a festive dance with the men that lasted long into the night.

* * *

After the wedding Behr began to work as a shochet (ritual slaughterer) in the employ of Rabbi Salanter, and Nesha began keeping house in a bare one-room apartment.

During the first weeks of their married life, Behr spent a lot of time getting his papers. "Papers" meant a residence permit giving him and his family the right to live in Memel. The city was under Prussian rule, while the tsar of Russia ruled over the surrounding villages. When Behr arrived, he was considered a Russian immigrant, just as Nesha's parents were when they arrived. Nesha could still remember her father sighing at the table and saying, "Thank God we have our papers." Jews had been in Memel since around the beginning of the nineteenth century. But at first the right to settle there was given only to Jews who came from other cities in Prussia. Some of these Germanic Jews were wealthy merchants. Later East European Jews received the right to settle. But each new arrival had to go through a lengthy procedure before being awarded the precious papers.

With his papers in hand, Behr felt freer to think ahead. Every day, when he went to work, the salt breeze spoke to him: *You're on your way to America now.*

* * *

A man's affairs might well be beyond a woman's grasp, but still he had to live with his wife, and he couldn't live in silence. So Behr often told his thoughts to Nesha.

He told Nesha about his plan to emigrate. He didn't ask her for her own ideas on the subject. Why should he? A woman had to obey her husband. It was best to make her understand this from the start.

He tried to keep conversation to everyday, non-spiritual subjects. He told her very little about his studies at the yeshiva in Telz. The all-male yeshiva was not an appropriate subject to discuss with a woman. She asked about it once or twice, then gave up when he became monosyllabic.

"Your brother lives in Telz," she said, sensing that this was safer ground. *How nice it must have been for him not to be alone in a strange city.*

She waited, but Behr didn't say anything of the sort. This confused her. Did a boy never get homesick, as a girl would?

"My brother has no idea how to make a good living," Behr said. He shook his head disapprovingly.

"He just trades in grain and flax, when there are already too many grain dealers in Telz. Anybody can see that it's not a good line of work. He never will do any better, he'll just scrape by, for his whole life long."

Nesha decided to risk a few questions. "What is a good line of work?"

"Well, for instance, *shechitah*, animal slaughtering, which is, thank God, my profession now."

He spoke with pride, but she rewarded him only with a blank look. Behr saw the question in her eyes.

"Ignorant people think it is like butchering. But a butcher doesn't need an education. A shochet has to know the laws, because if he makes an error, then the entire carcass cannot be used. And he has to examine the animal for what the law calls 'sickness defects,' which would make the whole animal unfit to eat."

Nesha imagined a man bringing his sick cow to be slaughtered, waiting anxiously in the butcher shop. And then the shochet would shake his head and say, "Unfit to eat!" It was hard enough on a poor family when a chicken they paid for was unfit to eat.

"A shochet has to inspire confidence in his clients," Behr continued. "To show that he knows the laws."

"Did you learn that in Telz too?"

"Of course, where else?" said Behr. "I took lessons during the afternoons when most of the boys just stole a quick nap. Because my father said that our rabbi needed a shochet he could trust."

Behr was always pleased with himself when he remembered how clever he had been, in letting himself be guided by his father's chance remark about the rabbi. *He'd made sure of finding employment in Memel after his studies, by learning a profession that made him useful to his rabbi. He'd made himself useful in another way too. The rabbi needed him to bolster up his floundering Talmud study group. The group met in the evenings when the men were tired from a hard workday. At twenty-three Behr had boundless energy and was a great student of Talmud; the rabbi could count on him. Of course, this was not something a woman would understand.*

"So when I finished my studies I came to Memel," Behr said. "And Rabbi Salanter, long life to him, helped me, not only with work, but in finding a match with a virtuous young woman."

Nesha smiled shyly. This was how he spoke of his marriage even when he was talking to Nesha herself.

Did he notice that she had big blue eyes with long, modest-looking dark eyelashes? And that she kept her beautiful brown hair clean and fragrant under the head covering that she wore whenever she went out? Most of her married girlfriends neglected their hair, since nobody but their husbands would ever see their heads uncovered. They even wore a kerchief at home in the evening, where it was not required unless there were guests, in order to hide their unkempt hair until their husbands came to them in bed in the dark.

"Do you know yet when we'll be going to America?" asked Nesha. The question had nothing to do with his last remark, but he did not seem to notice.

"It might take two or three years to save enough money for the trip," said Behr. "And besides, I want to wait until conditions are right."

"Of course," she said, though she had no idea what he meant. *Oh no*, she thought. *This means we will have to visit his parents in Salant.* The thought of visiting her mother-in-law, Kuna, terrified her. A teacher's wife with two scholars for sons was sure to be more learned than her own mother, and ultra-strict in religious observance. Would she take Nesha into the kitchen and interrogate her?

The visit itself, a few months later, was even worse than she imagined. Mother-in-law Kuna was a massive woman with a face that seemed hard as iron. She tested her daughter-in-law on how to prepare a chicken correctly, then embarrassed her by asking if she knew the rules about keeping herself clean, in particular her most intimate parts. How to tell when it was time for her to go the *mikvah* for her monthly immersion in the ritual bath, and how to prepare for the immersion.

After a few hours of this Nesha fled to the back yard. There she leaned against a big laundry tub until she stopped shaking. *I'll make a vow right now*, she thought, then hesitated, trembling: was a woman allowed to make a vow? Just in case, she spit on the ground three times, right, left, and right, to confound the evil eye. Then she said aloud, but softly: "Never, never in my whole life will I treat my daughter-in-law so cruelly as I have been treated today."

Nesha felt better immediately. She straightened up and headed back to the house.

At the doorway she nearly collided with her mother-in-law, who'd evidently been spying on her, though thankfully from too far off to hear her words. "Have you been vomiting your breakfast?" Kuna said sternly. And then, less sternly, "Might you be, God willing, in a family way?"

Nesha's hand flew to her stomach. She had not intended to deceive her mother-in-law, but she quickly realized the advantages of the deception.

"I think I might be," she said sweetly. It wasn't a lie, she reasoned, because in truth she might be. During two weeks of every month, she might become pregnant.

Her mother-in-law beamed. "God willing," she repeated, wiping her hands on her apron. "Now, come in and we'll deal with that chicken together."

After that, the woman's behavior changed for the better. Even so, Nesha sighed in relief when the visit was over and the wagon took her and Behr back to Memel.

Nesha wasn't pregnant. But two months later she really was pregnant, and by the time Behr wrote to his parents about it her mother-in-law had no doubt forgotten the exact date and would never confront Nesha with her little lie.

Talking with her husband was sometimes worse than visiting her mother-in-law. He had such a stern, formal way of speaking to her, like a rabbi.

In fact, he was a rabbi, since he had completed his yeshiva studies with the final qualification called *smichah*. If he wanted to, he could go to a village and serve as rabbi to a whole community. He would never do this, but he spoke in the authoritative voice of a rabbi, even at home.

Sometimes, at the end of a Sabbath meal, if there was no male guest for him to converse with, he lectured Nesha on a simple religious theme.

"Rabbi Salanter is a great man, a great scholar," he said. "The rabbi teaches us to look at learning in a new way," he said. "The new way is called Musar, which means concentrating on morals, that is, on moral improvement. That is the real purpose of Torah study."

The renowned rabbi had been very critical of the studies in the yeshiva, which he said were often little more than theological quibbling. Of course, Behr softened this, so as not to sound too critical.

"What the rabbi says is that the modern yeshiva must aim at improving a man's character through study," he said. "Not only at memorizing the law."

Nesha listened quietly. It was pleasant to hear pious words at the table.

Behr became a different person whenever he discussed how things were made—carriages or grinding mills, whatever. Then he waxed so enthusiastic that he forgot his wife was only a woman who could not always understand what he was saying. Once the shoemaker had shown him an advertisement for a machine in France that could make shoes, "a hundred pairs of shoes, in the same time it takes to make just one pair with a peg and awl." He tried to explain exactly how the machine worked.

It seemed as if she had married two different men—a stern scholar and an enthusiastic boy.

On good days, it amused her. On other days, when he was in his grim didactic mood, she had to hide her frustration behind a submissive exterior. Otherwise, he would explode in anger.

Luckily she was good at her job. She had learned as a girl that it was a woman's task to make harmony at home, *shelom bayis*, which literally meant "peace in the house." Her mother had endlessly drilled her in this. Now she knew how vital it was.

Nesha gave birth to their first baby, a girl, the following March. The delivery was easy, for a first baby. Amidst praise from the midwife and her mother—for she had done well and scarcely cried out—Nesha held the baby out for Behr to see as soon as she was safely swaddled.

"Look at those little fingers," he said, taking them in his big ones, entirely forgetting his disappointment that the baby was a girl. He had never been so near a tiny baby before. "And fingernails. How great is the Lord's work," he said.

"A first girl is a sign of many sons to come," said Nesha's mother, as soon as there were no men present in the room.

"What does that mean, Mama?"

"It's just something that everyone says when you have a daughter first."

Maybe there's more to it, Nesha thought. Maybe God wanted a woman who was destined to have a big family to have a daughter first of all. That way, the daughter would be able to help her at home. It made sense, didn't it?

She asked Behr about it, right before the naming ceremony, but regretted it instantly. He frowned and answered sharply. "That is foolishness, women's talk. Children are God's will, to question His purpose is irreligious."

He saw her shamefaced look and stopped. His wife would learn to watch her words.

They named the baby Mirale.

While Nesha was occupied with her role as mother, Behr continued to work as shochet. Rabbi Salanter left Memel in 1882 for Paris. He told his many friends and supporters that he hoped to bring a revival of religious fervor to the Jewish community there, as he had done in Memel. "Such an old man, to begin life in a new city!" Nesha exclaimed when Behr told her this. Fortunately Behr's work was not affected, for the rabbi left him with enough clients in Memel.

The next year Nesha gave birth to a boy. The baby, a sturdy, ruddy-faced infant, received the name of Meyer. Behr was delighted with his son. He spoke formally about the blessing of a son, while his blue eyes sparkled with pleasure.

The following year, Nesha had a miscarriage, but it was an early one, so she recovered quickly and without too much distress. She was soon pregnant again. In July of 1885, she gave birth to another boy, who was given the name of Jacob.

What a beautiful baby, she thought, as she took him in her arms for the very first time. The baby's dark hair curled softly over his little forehead. He had a wise look on his little face, and he wasn't constantly squalling, the way her first boy baby had done. Nesha fondled the tiny hands, feeling warm and proud and exultant. *He looks like he has dreams in his little head, like Jacob the dreamer*, she thought. She did not say this aloud. Then another idea came into her mind.

"Do you think I am becoming a mother of many sons, just like in the saying?" she asked her mother.

This time her mother made a sharp gesture with her hand, and answered crossly, "Hush, do you want to bring on the evil eye?"

Nesha was silent. She pressed her lips together in frustration. Why shouldn't she rejoice in bearing sons? Was she not supposed to have any feelings at all? And another thing—when would she bring her sons to America? Hadn't Behr as good as promised it to her?

The three years of Behr's promise had ended, and they were still in Memel. An expulsion edict was once again hovering over the Jews who did not have Prussian citizenship, and Rabbi Ruelf was once again trying to negotiate a compromise.

Behr told her not to worry. Did he know something that he wasn't telling her?

Finally, just after the holidays, came the opportunity that Behr was waiting for.

A group of family friends from Salant living in Cincinnati wrote to Behr's father to offer Behr a job, because their shochet had died. Behr showed Nesha the letter, which was written in Yiddish:

> . . . in Cincinnati we have a growing number of families from Salant. Our shochet, Reb David, may his soul rest in peace, has died and he is much missed by our community. We need a man well versed in *shechitah*, one who is learned and trustworthy. Reb Simon Isaacs agreed with me that we should write you to advise your son, Behr, of our position. Also the butcher, Israel Oscherowitz . . .

The letter was signed Rabbi Elya Hilkowitz. The same letter also offered a position as butcher to Israel Oscherowitz, a friend of Behr's, also living in Memel. Behr and his friend did not hesitate for a moment in accepting the offer.

Not a day too soon! With winter approaching, Behr wasted no time; he made a steamship booking within the month. Both families were to leave on the same ship, on the third Monday of November 1885.

On Saturday night Nesha packed the clothes they had worn on the Sabbath, and the candlesticks and other special items that were only used on the Sabbath. She did some more packing on Sunday night. She packed the last items, their blanket, towels, and pots and dishes, early on Monday morning, after serving a hasty breakfast.

The grocer lent them his handcart for the morning. His assistant would meet them at the port and take it back to the shop.

By mid-morning, all of their bags were loaded on the cart, and two-year-old Meyer was seated on top. Nesha held baby Jacob balanced on her hip, and took her little girl, Mirale, by the hand.

Behr pushed the cart, and from that moment on, he focused only on the task at hand. Memel had only been a stopover on his way to America. A long stopover, with a wife and three children added to his baggage, but a stopover just the same.

It was quite another matter for Nesha. This was her home-town, and she was walking on streets she knew intimately, past familiar shops and houses and doorways which she had known since she was a small child.

Her heart leaped up at the enormity of what she was doing.

"God bless you!" "A safe journey!" Her friends called out, as she passed. Some came out to embrace her, and her best friends gave her small gifts to remember them by. Feigel gave her a woolen headscarf, which she had worked on for weeks. Shayna gave her a small bag containing a few carved wooden toys to amuse the children on the boat. Nesha stowed the gifts carefully inside one of the bundles on top of the cart.

The entire neighborhood stood at doors and windows watching them. What were they thinking? That Nesha was a lucky young woman? Or that she and her husband were fools?

Only last week the rabbi at their neighborhood synagogue had spoken against emigration. He had said: "A Jew should not even move from Laizuva to Molotoi unless it is God's will." Laizuva and Molotoi were villages. Why shouldn't a Jew move from one village to another?

Nesha had waited until the Sabbath was over to hear what Behr would say about it at home. She was sure he thought it was a foolish statement. And it had been aimed directly at Behr. The whole congregation knew that by the next Sabbath Behr and his family would be aboard ship. But Behr had said nothing, in order not to speak ill of the rabbi.

Now at last they were on their way.

Nesha felt as if she were skipping along, although anyone who saw her would have seen just a heavily burdened young mother, her waist already a little thick after bearing three children, trudging along a few steps behind her husband.

The two older children felt her joy, and were joyful with her, understanding nothing but their mother's excitement. They held onto her hands, and feared nothing at all in this world, for no faith is so absolute as a small child's faith in its mother when she is happy and confident.

They did not even notice the black, churning water below them as they followed Behr up the gangway.

* * *

Yes, the moment of embarking was wonderful. But once on board, Nesha's life was a constant torment. The three children were hers alone, it seemed—Behr was somehow absent. Of course, this had often been the case at home. But the life of a family on shipboard was reduced to its most basic elements: one man, one woman, three children, their feeding and physical needs.

The smallest member of the family, baby Jacob, had the fewest needs. Nesha had plenty of milk in her breasts. She nursed him distractedly and laid him in a pile of bedding at her side, then focused on her husband and toddlers. Each day was harder than the previous one.

They had to get off the first ship when they reached Hamburg. This meant packing everything up again, and trudging down another long, shaky gangplank to the dock. There was no respite while they were on shore. Nesha had to mind the children and keep them occupied for hours in the port area, while Behr tried to negotiate for them to board the America-bound steamer immediately, so as not to waste precious money on lodgings at an inn.

The long hours ashore in Hamburg—in a bone-chilling autumn wind—were enough for the children's feet to become adjusted to walking on solid ground again. They whined pitifully when they found themselves climbing back up another gangplank, for this time they knew what awaited them.

Before Nesha could settle in, Behr decided that their allotted space was unsatisfactory, so he went to negotiate for a better one. By the time she was able to unpack and create some order in their new space, both the older children were crying. Then a storm blew in, and the ship rocked, and they all vomited. Nesha had not imagined it could be so difficult to endure.

She had to prepare meals and serve them to her family, all in the crowded space allotted to them. She had to nurse the baby even while she was seasick, with everyone crowded around her. She slept very little because the children slept fitfully, and cried out loud each time the movements of the ship jerked them out of their dreams.

Nesha's few possessions kept getting used up, or ruined, or lost. One of her cooking pots was missing, and none of their fellow travelers admitted to having seen it. Meyer decided to use his mother's precious new scarf to vomit into, so that it was completely ruined.

Little Mirale lost the small bag with the wooden toys. "Where is it?" Nesha cried out, but the frightened girl would not answer until she threatened to slap her.

"A big girl gave me a silver ring for it," the little girl confessed, "but it broke." The trembling child held out a broken bauble that was apparently the "silver" ring. And now the bag, Nesha's very last gift from home, was gone forever.

"Silver ring, oh yes, of course! You're a wicked child is all!" Nesha shouted. The little girl crawled into a corner to cry. Nesha turned to fuss with her pots, hiding the fact that she was nearly crying herself. *God,* she thought. *How much can one woman endure?*

Of course, she was young, or she would have realized that a woman can endure much more than that.

During the second week the baby, Jacob, became very ill. Nesha could not tell exactly when the illness started. He wailed endlessly with what seemed to be colic, or perhaps it was a fever. Meanwhile the two other children were constantly fidgeting and complaining, and there were no more toys to distract them. The whining only stopped when they slept, and she slept heavily herself, so heavily that Behr could not budge her. This went on for several days, while the baby moaned constantly. Behr sat alongside them with a book, giving his flustered wife occasional looks that told her louder than words: *you should manage better.*

Nesha's nerves were increasingly frazzled. On the third day of the children's endless whining over the background of the sick baby's wails, she shouted at Behr. He responded promptly by taking a prayer book and withdrawing to a quiet corner on the deck. Without his threatening presence, the children's whining became louder. They screamed and she slapped them, and then they whimpered so annoyingly that she slapped them again. When she fed them porridge it stuck to the pot and to their clothing and faces. And in between all of this, she breastfed the baby. But it sucked only weakly, irritably, and she was so weak and tired herself—perhaps she did not try hard enough. Or perhaps, not often enough. When she lay the baby down, he wailed weakly. A thin yellowish liquid was all that came out of his body when she changed the cloth that wrapped him.

On the following morning the wailing stopped.

The baby Jacob lay on his makeshift pile of bedding for hours, with half-opened eyes. He ignored her breast when she presented it. She laid him back down on the bedding and looked around despairingly. Where was anyone who could tell her what to do? Could this nightmare really be happening to her?

"I think they're going to lose that one," said an older woman, a stranger whose family shared the close quarters with Nesha's family.

At that, Nesha picked up the baby again, and tried to wake him. "My Jacob, my precious one," she said, and pinched his pale sunken cheeks, while Behr (who was back in the family space now) watched her. The baby remained apathetic.

Behr said, "I think it may be God's will that we lose this one."

Another hour or two passed, and the baby did not improve. His little arms lay slack, like a puppet's. His breathing slowed down, then became irregular and barely noticeable. Nesha took the baby in her lap and watched each movement of the little chest, as though watching it might somehow help to keep it moving up and down.

When she looked up, Behr was no longer at her side. He was a few steps away talking softly with his friend, Mr. Oscherowitz. "We will need some linen for the shroud," he was saying. She looked hopelessly at the unmoving baby in her arms.

And then suddenly it was all too much for her. Mrs. Oscherowitz was at her side. "Please take the baby for a while," Nesha whispered to her hoarsely. As soon as the baby was out of her hands, she stood up and took a few steps away toward the railing. All she wanted in this world was to breathe some fresh air, which she did, in big gulps.

Minutes later, Behr returned with the linen shroud and prepared to wrap the baby, who lay motionless in Mrs. Oscherowitz's lap. A small crowd had gathered to join Behr in prayer, and preparations were being made alongside the railing. Burial on board ship meant sliding the body down a wooden chute into the sea. Nesha's eyes were too filled with tears to notice the details.

And then Mrs. Oscherowitz's sharp voice cut through the heaviness of the grief-laden air. "Wait, I think the baby is breathing!"

The crowd standing at the rail was suddenly hushed. Perhaps, like Nesha, they were each holding their breath. In the silence, a tiny whimper came from the little bundle. "Blessed is the Lord our God, healer of the sick," said Behr in a shaky voice. A dozen or so voices answered "Amen." Nesha's throat was too choked up for her to join them.

The people who had witnessed the miracle crowded closer to see. Mrs. Oscherowitz looked as happy as anyone who has just played a role in saving a life. She smiled and spoke softly to the baby. In a moment, he opened his eyes and coughed. The crowd watched motionless, as his breathing became more regular. Nesha held out her trembling arms to receive him, then sat down abruptly, her knees too wobbly to stand.

She nursed him briefly, still shaking. He accepted a few drops of milk and the remainder spilled gloriously all over his face. Behr grabbed the shroud and threw it quickly overboard, lest it bring bad luck.

Within minutes, the baby's color improved ever so slightly.

He nursed a little more each day and made a complete recovery.

*　*　*

For days afterwards, Nesha was restless. "I should have been holding the baby myself," she said to Behr. As soon as she spoke, she regretted it.

Behr scowled. "The baby is well, thank God. What are you talking about?"

After that Nesha kept her thoughts to herself. She would never mention the incident to anybody, ever again, for the rest of her life, but Mrs. Oscherowitz, who was not bound to secrecy, would eventually reveal it.

But the silence surrounding the incident was not enough to blot it out of Nesha's mind. *Was she a bad mother?* The question tormented her, and there was nobody she could confide in—certainly not her husband. How could she expect him to understand? The holy books advised men to avoid women's talk.

Her whole life long, everything had been done for her, she had followed the rules and known what to do. She had been an obedient child. She had married the man her parents had chosen for her. She had borne children.

Yet look what had happened. The very first time she was faced with a real question of life or death, she had failed miserably. She had left the miracle of her baby's life in another woman's hands. All her years of learning to cook and clean and to care for a home had not been enough.

How could she face her life in America, now that she knew how weak she was? When she saw the port of the New World approaching, she felt more fear than joy.

Chapter 2

On Dry Land

How many levels of favor has the Omnipresent One bestowed upon us:

If He had brought us out from Egypt, and had not carried out judgments against them, it would have sufficed us!

If He had carried out judgments against them, and not against their idols, it would have sufficed us!

If He had destroyed their idols, and had not smitten their first-born, it would have sufficed us!

If He had smitten their first-born, and had not given us their wealth, it would have sufficed us!

If He had given us their wealth, and had not split the sea for us, it would have sufficed us!

If He had split the sea for us, and had not taken us through it on dry land, it would have sufficed us!

If He had taken us through the sea on dry land, and had not drowned our oppressors in it, it would have sufficed us!

—Passover Haggadah

The ship landed in New York on the seventeenth of December 1885 with its cargo of immigrants. Along with a hundred other weary families, Dov Behr, his wife, and their three small children waited in a big immigration hall for processing. When their turn came, an official noted the date and some other information on their document of arrival, stamped it, and handed it over. Behr held the precious document up high for Nesha to see.

Manischewitz, she read. The unfamiliar name stood out in fresh black ink.

"Look, Nesha, this is our name in America. May God grant us prosperity with it!"

Her husband's face was framed by his tousled black hair, black cap, and beard. In the tall windows of the immigration hall behind him, the sun shone brightly.

"Amen!" she answered.

It was a magic moment, and she sensed that somehow their new name was a part of it. Young men in Lithuania often changed their names, to obtain their papers or to escape twenty years of service in the tsar's army. So it hadn't surprised her when she saw that the name she had glimpsed several times on Behr's documents was different from his father's name. Behr had not given his wife any reason for the change.

"Behr—" she began, but it was hardly the moment for explanations. He had already stuffed the document deep inside his coat and was asking a second official, in words and gestures, to direct him to the train station.

They hastened off in that direction with their baggage, joined by the Oscherowitz family. Each person's thoughts now were on their common destination: the city named Cincinnati, where jobs awaited their men. *How lucky we are to have a destination.* The thought went through their minds as they made their way through the crowd of immigrants who were mostly just milling around the port area like lost sheep.

The journey by train was another trial, but Nesha was learning to deal with her trials somewhat better now. She slapped the children less often, and held baby Jacob in her arms gratefully, tenderly, even when he cried. "My precious one," she whispered into the baby's ear," her voice masked by the clattering of the wheels, "I will always take such good care of you."

In a few days it was over and they stood together in the bustling Cincinnati station, among dozens of other new arrivals, all looking hopelessly rumpled and unwashed. Some local people stood around staring at them. Trains bearing dozens of odd-looking immigrants were still a relative novelty here. Behr's threadbare black coat had been so clean when she laid it out for him in Memel, and now it was a desperate-looking, dirty shade of gray. There was nothing to be done for it. Nesha waited wearily, with the soiled baby in her arms and the tired, grimy little girl at her side.

At last two representatives of the local Lithuanian Jewish community appeared to greet them. One of them went over to Mr. Oscherowitz. The other approached Behr, his hand extended.

"Welcome to our city and our community," the man said. "I trust you have had a good journey."

It was wonderful to hear the words of welcome, and the familiar accent. The man did not shake Nesha's hand—this was not allowed among the pious—and anyway, she was holding the baby. He spoke only to Behr.

"The community has found an apartment for you" were his next words.

Nesha squeezed her little girl's hand and whispered, "We'll be home soon." At this, the tired child perked up a little. The two men loaded the baggage onto a waiting wagon that conveyed them a few short city blocks to a three-story tenement building. The men carried the bags and bundles up a dark, narrow staircase.

"Here you are," said the man, this time including Nesha in his glance.

The tiny apartment was equipped with a few basic furnishings and household supplies. "We've obtained some children's clothing for you from one of the Jewish charities," the man said, pointing to a bundle on the table. He said a few words to Behr in the doorway and left. What a relief it was to put the children into clean clothing! They let themselves be changed as limply as rag dolls.

When this was done, the entire family sank gratefully onto the unmoving mattresses.

* * *

The pale winter sun had scarcely found its way to the bare, mottled window of their new home when another member of the community arrived to accompany Behr to his new place of work. Later in the morning, the rabbi's wife came to visit Nesha.

"Please come in, um—" Nesha hesitated over the correct form of address.

"Call me just rebbetzin," said her visitor. "Bless us, we don't need to be so formal as the men." And the rabbi's wife—the rebbetzin—sat down on the stiff wooden chair that Nesha extended to her. She must have found it comfortable enough, for she stayed most of the morning.

Nesha made some tea and served it. The children had revived somewhat since yesterday, but they were still subdued. The older two sat quietly on the floor, nibbling on some hard biscuits. Baby Jacob lay quietly on a blanket.

The rebbetzin hadn't been in America very long, and most of her information concerned the Jewish community. Nesha listened eagerly.

"The Jews of Cincinnati are very divided in their synagogues," she said.

"First there is our own synagogue, which belongs to the Jews of the entire Kovno region of Lithuania, as well as Memel. There is another synagogue of East European Jews, bigger than ours. Plus there is another smaller one, and there is also a Polish one." She gave the names of each of these, plus the rabbis' names. "And then there are the German Jews, who have been in Cincinnati much longer, and they have their own synagogues. But several of their biggest synagogues are not real synagogues at all, they are of the Reformed persuasion."

Nesha was puzzled by the word. The rebbetzin explained. "It means that in those synagogues even the rabbi does not keep the Jewish laws, not even the Sabbath, God forbid."

Was she joking?

"Maybe what you mean is that the rabbis aren't strict enough," Nesha suggested. "Like some of the German rabbis back home, before Rabbi Ruelf." The German rabbi in Memel—the previous one, whose name she did not remember—had been a pious man, but he wasn't strict enough with his congregation. The Jewish merchants used to go the port on the Sabbath to supervise the loading and unloading of goods. When Rabbi Salanter arrived in Memel, he put a stop to this, even though he wasn't the chief rabbi of the community. He had publicly scolded the people who did it until eventually they were ashamed and stopped.

Modern, assimilated German Jews—this was something Nesha knew about.

But the rebbetzin said no, here it was different. In Cincinnati, the rabbis themselves walked around with their heads uncovered, and they had given a banquet a couple of years ago where they had served non-kosher food.

"Crabs, and shrimp, too! And afterwards they said it was a mistake!"

She folded her arms and leaned back, with the air of having proven her case.

Nesha wondered whether to believe the story.

When the rebbetzin left, Nesha made a simple lunch for the children and went about her afternoon cheerfully. The children played quietly, reacting as always to her tranquil mood, and the baby took a long nap. She hummed as she prepared the evening meal and waited for Behr.

He returned at dusk, somewhat less elated than his wife after his first day's experience.

Before he spoke he dropped a large bundle down beside the door. Then he sat down heavily and waited for her to serve him a glass of tea.

With the steaming tea in front of him, he began to relax a little.

"I have seen my workplace, and we will have, thank God, a living," he said.

The man who had come to meet him in the morning had started by showing him around his work area. Mr. Oscherowitz, who would be doing the butchering, joined them for this part of the introduction. They would be working closely together, since Behr's job as shochet involved only the actual slaughtering. Slaughtering was more important, for there were minute laws on how it should be done so that the animals would not suffer. But butchering involved a lot of heavy work, cutting up parts of animals to make them attractive and salable. As it happened, two big carcasses had arrived yesterday and were ready for chopping. Seeing an apron and some more or less adequate tools, the butcher had rolled up his sleeves and gone right to work.

The two other men left Mr. Oscherowitz in the shop and entered a small side room, which served as an office.

And then the community representative said to Behr: "The rabbi says to tell you right from the start, this is not a rich community. You'll need to supplement your job with some peddling, like all of us do."

While Behr digested this unwelcome piece of news, the man explained further. The men who made up the Kovno community had discussed Behr's situation long before his arrival.

"We made all the arrangements for you," the man said, clearly expecting praise for their foresight. "So I can already give you some tea and spices on consignment." At this, the man indicated a rather large bundle on the floor beside them.

Behr was silent a moment. There was no way of refusing the offer. He was entirely dependent on the community and was not about to offend them on the first day. He stifled his disappointment, thanked the man for his support, and shook hands with him on it. When he left, he took the bundle and mumbled his thanks once more.

"And so your husband is a tea and spice peddler," Behr concluded. "As you can see for yourself." He pointed to the bundle by the door. "It's a start, nothing more."

"God willing." Nesha rose quickly to rescue the spices from two-year-old Meyer, who had discovered this treasure while they talked, and was curiously examining a packet of tea, trying to open it with his chubby fingers.

The little boy protested, and his sister Mirale chimed in, and soon Nesha had her hands full, with the children to placate and dinner to prepare.

* * *

It was December, a grim time to be a poor immigrant family in a strange city. Privately, Nesha wondered whether they would have managed to keep going at all if not for the charitable societies. The society members were mostly older German Jewish women who'd been in America many years and were so assimilated that they seemed like real Americans to Nesha. Women who were not wealthy themselves participated in its work by gathering used clothing from wealthier families and mending it for the use of the poor.

A woman from the charitable society knocked on Nesha's door early one morning, just after Behr had left for work. Nesha greeted her with a questioning look.

"Hello, are you Mrs. Nesha Manischewitz?" she asked in German, stumbling a little over the name. "I'm Henrietta Quitman, from the Benevolent Society. We brought you a bundle last week and I want to know if there is anything else we can do for you."

Nesha blushed, at the same time motioning Henrietta into the room. The woman spoke German oddly, but she could be understood.

"No, you were very generous," she said with a shy smile. "We do not need anything." Of course, this was not true—any casual visitor could see that they still needed many things. "But please come in and sit down."

Henrietta took the chair that was offered her. And at that moment the little figure of Mirale advanced curiously toward her, looking quite angelic in a dress that trailed to the floor. "What a pretty little girl you are!" Henrietta held out her arms to the child.

In an instant she whipped out a piece of string and expertly measured the little girl, replacing the string in a pocket just as quickly. Mirale smiled shyly at the stranger and offered her a biscuit from a small, damp fist.

Henrietta promised to return with another bundle, which she did, a few days later.

And then the months from December to April rushed by, while Behr worked hard at his two jobs and Nesha kept house and cooked and occupied the children as best as she could.

She kept her despair on hold as she frantically prepared for the Passover holiday. How she would have loved to welcome the holiday with new things! Wealthy families kept an entire set of pots and dishes just to use on the Passover holidays: bright, shiny pots that never saw a crumb of bread, waiting all year in a cupboard to welcome the bread-free holiday like soldiers marching out in shiny new armor. Instead, on top of all the other cleaning of the shabby apartment, she had to scour the old pots that would not shine with cleanliness no matter how hard she tried.

Like an angel, the charity woman Henrietta appeared at her door a week before the holiday. This time she found Nesha flushed and tired, and the little apartment in total disorder, with pots on the floor and signs of frantic housecleaning. "Passover,"

Nesha said, waving at the room apologetically. The assimilated Henrietta had no idea of the frantic cleaning a pious woman must do on the eve of Passover, but it was not hard to take in the situation.

"Tell me honestly what you need," she said.

Nesha was too tired to protest. "I guess there are a few things," she admitted.

Behr had asked for an advance on his pay, just to cover the cost of food and candles and soap for the holiday. But there were other items, and Nesha named them, hesitantly.

Henrietta brought these things the next day, along with an extra gift: a curtain that was just right for the small window, to give the bare apartment a more festive look.

The gifts were a *mechayeh*, literally a breath of fresh life. Nesha hung the curtain on the window the moment Henrietta left, and sat down to admire it.

She was beginning—just beginning—to feel hopeful.

Even so, at the first Passover Seder dinner, Behr was gloomy, and the two older children, taking their cue from him, took no pleasure in the ceremony. Behr read the beautiful words of the Haggadah, telling the whole story of the holiday—the exodus from Egypt, the unleavened bread, the manna in the desert. He read it all the way through, and all the special foods were set before him on the table as decreed by the tradition, even though the children were too small to understand. For as Nesha well knew, the whole Passover story must be told anyway, in every Jewish home. The text itself said so: "Even if all of us were wise, all of us understanding, all of us knowing the Torah, we would still be obligated to discuss the exodus from Egypt; and everyone who discusses the exodus from Egypt at length is praiseworthy."

But the familiar words of the Passover story lacked some of their luster this year. And the second night, when the Seder ceremony was repeated, it was the same. The children—sensing their father's mood, as children often do—fidgeted and misbehaved, and teased the baby to make him cry.

* * *

Nesha received another visit from Henrietta in August. By this time Nesha was counting on the older woman for advice. And why not? The only other person giving her advice was the rebbetzin. And Nesha was beginning to realize that the rebbetzin did not know much more about American life than she did. Nesha gratefully welcomed her guest and they sat down to drink a glass of water with lemon. Nesha hoped Henrietta didn't mind that the water was not as cool as it should be. Cincinnati was sweltering hot in August, and she already owed money to the iceman.

"There's a kindergarten at the public school," Henrietta said. "And you should take your girl Mirale over there as soon as it opens in September. She is nearly old enough, you must ask them if they will accept her."

Nesha hesitated.

"Behr says he's hoping next year we will have enough children for a Jewish school, and if they can get a teacher, and if all the congregations can agree on it—"

Her voice trailed off. *The Jewish school might only be for boys*, she was thinking. Behr hadn't said much about it yet—it was really just an idea.

Henrietta saw her wavering.

"Well, you know, Nesha, your little girl needs to learn English while she's still small. It will be much easier for her. Then she'll be like a real American girl." Henrietta smiled.

"It doesn't matter so much for a girl, does it?" Nesha's question was addressed more to herself than to Henrietta. It was the same as in Europe, after all. Jewish girls in even the most pious families were often sent to a public school. It was the boys who needed to read Hebrew and study the holy books.

She nodded shyly.

"That's settled, then." Henrietta went on to her next suggestion.

"At the public school, they don't like to use foreign names. What can we think of for her American name? It should start with the same letter as her Jewish name."

She made it sound like a game. The two women went through several of Henrietta's suggestions until they finally decided on "Mayme."

Mayme. What would Behr say?

Perhaps she would tell just a tiny lie—she would tell him that the law required it.

Nesha was already pregnant again, although not noticeably. She smiled as she began to grasp what sending her little girl to school would mean to her: she would have one less child to watch during her pregnancy.

And by next spring little Mirale—Mayme—would know English well enough to understand the shopkeepers and interpret for her mother.

* * *

Nesha's fourth child was born in January 1887. It was an easy delivery, and it was another boy. They named him Joseph. Three sons already—Behr was delighted. "Another son, may he live a long life of success, learning, and *mitzvos*!

He always said this on the birth of a son.

"God willing," Nesha answered, as she always did. And she leaned back on the pillows. She enjoyed lying in with a new baby—it was so brief, and she would be so busy when she arose from her bed.

She mused over Behr's blessing and the explanation he had given her when their first son was born. There were 613 religious commandments, or *mitzvos*. Some were negative, which meant they required one not to do something, like not eating pork. The rest were positive, requiring one to do something, like honoring parents or observing the Sabbath. Everyone had to obey the negative commandments. Most of the positive commandments were equally binding on all. But because women had their own natural rhythm of life, they were exempt from those positive commandments that had to be accomplished at a specific time or season, such as praying three times daily. Unlike a daughter, a son would have the opportunity, and the duty, of keeping *all* of the *mitzvos*.

She made a mental note to explain these things to Henrietta after the lying-in. Her friend was sure to arrive with a gift for the new baby.

Even with pleasant thoughts on her mind, it was a real effort for Nesha to get back on her feet again. She needed to, though, for on the eighth day there was the circumcision ceremony, which meant she must make the apartment and the children presentable.

Unlike Nesha, Behr was always full of energy after a birth in the family. As soon as the dishes from the circumcision party were cleared away, he began inquiring solicitously about her recovery. He asked her about the postpartum bleeding. "Has it stopped completely, as I hope it has?" he asked. He knew he could rely on his wife to examine herself carefully, the way she had undoubtedly learned from her mother, to determine when the bleeding had stopped. According to the law, she could begin counting clean days starting as early as the fifth day after the birth of a boy, on condition that the bleeding had stopped, or from the seventh day after the birth of a girl.

He waited another week while she counted seven clean days, as required. Only after the counting was completed, was she allowed to visit the community's ritual bath, the *mikvah*, where she would make herself pure from head to toe in flowing water. Until then, her husband was forbidden to touch her.

"If you feel that you are, um, ready to go out," Behr said on the morning of the seventh day of counting, "I'll watch the children this evening."

Nesha blushed, understanding the reference. *He was eager to come to her in bed.* So among all her other duties, she managed to make an visit to the *mikvah* that evening. That made her pure, so that Behr could have his need fulfilled.

* * *

The second Passover, in the spring of 1887, was a big improvement over the first one. The table looked more festive, set for the ceremony with all the traditional foods on a new china plate: three whole matzos, a roasted shankbone, a roasted egg, a horseradish, charoses (a mixture of apples, wine, and nuts), and some celery for dipping in salt water.

A delicious aroma came from the kitchen, so that the older children wriggled in anticipation of the meal that would be served as soon as their father got to the words *shulchan orech*, the phrase in the Haggadah signifying that it was time to lay the table.

Best of all, on the table was some delicious raisin wine that lent a heavenly sweetness to the evening. Everyone was required to drink four cups of wine at the Passover Seder, poured out by Behr at the appointed intervals during the reading of the Haggadah.

Behr waited until everyone's eyes were on him—and his own blue eyes sparkled with pleasure—then solemnly recited the blessing, "Blessed are You, Lord our God, King of the universe, who creates the fruit of the vine."

Then there was blessed silence as they all tasted the wine. A brother of a cousin of Behr's had made this raisin wine with Ohio grapes just before the holiday. It was called Flengyaner after the name of the region in Europe where this kind of wine was a specialty. The children, awed by the ceremony, which actually gave them the right to taste the precious drink in their own little glasses, sipped the wine (diluted by Nesha) with pride, and their wide eyes reflected the sparkle of the ruby liquid.

The wine was served at each meal, so that its sweet taste stayed in their mouths and the lighthearted mood continued throughout the holiday.

The in-between days of the holiday were the most relaxed. They were not full holidays with all of the work restrictions that a full holiday implied. On the in-between days Nesha did not have to be so careful in the kitchen—she could use the cook stove freely, and light up a new fire to boil hot water to wash the pots, instead of carefully transferring an existing fire, as she had to do on a full holiday.

Behr worked half-days, and came home at lunchtime. He rolled up his sleeves at the table, his work day over.

"After the holiday I'm going to do just a minimum of peddling, maybe nine or ten hours a week," he said on the third day. He paused to dip a piece of matzo into his tea.

Nesha looked at him expectantly.

"So far," he said, "our life here isn't so bad, but it isn't so good either. We're still the same as we were in Memel. If I do less peddling, maybe I can make another plan, do something else. By next Passover, God willing, I'll have something better."

He suddenly noticed Mirale hanging at his elbow, and popped the tea-sweetened matzo into her mouth. She swallowed it and laughed in surprise.

He smiled at her and said no more.

A week later, at the Havdalah ceremony that marked the end of the Sabbath, Behr finished the last drop of the wine.

He remained seated with the empty glass in his hand.

"That man made quite a profit with this wine," he said.

Nesha looked at him curiously. It was unusual for him to linger at the table after the ceremony was completed.

He set down the glass.

"The man is no fool. Selling a good product to Jews for Passover. You do a *mitzvah*, a good deed, and you make a profit too. People are willing to buy."

Nesha was drawn in by his enthusiasm.

"How true!" she exclaimed. "Just like me. Right before the holiday the rebbetzin's sister-in-law was selling such nice fruit preserves for the holiday, so I bought some, even though I had already spent too much. I thought, after all, it's for the holiday, for the children. To make the holiday sweet for them."

She paused to see how he took this confession. Just in case, she added, "Next year I'll plan better, I'll buy fruit when it's cheap and make my own preserves."

Behr nodded approvingly.

The moment seemed festive, though Nesha could not say why. How could she make it last a little longer? There were few possibilities, but she thought of one right away.

"Why don't you write a letter to your father, may he live to a hundred?"

It was the right suggestion, for a letter home should always be written when one is feeling optimistic. Behr rose immediately to bring paper and pen, while Nesha excitedly cleared the table.

Letters to his father were the only contact she had with family or friends in Europe. How had this happened? Her own father had been sickly for some time and no longer wrote. Her mother wasn't literate enough to write. Nesha did not correspond with her childhood girlfriends. There had been an unspoken understanding that the friendships would end with each one's marriage.

And so Behr sat down to write. He told his father about his work and the holiday. To Nesha's amusement, he even mentioned the Flengyaner wine. But he wrote this all in an academic, formal Hebrew that she could not begin to understand.

His father's letters were the same as Behr's —unreadable! Sometimes she wondered why she even bothered to encourage him to write. But she needed this contact with the Old Country, meager and second-hand as it was.

This evening, he let her add her own letter to his. She wrote in simple Yiddish:

Dearest father-in-law,
I thank you very much for your regards of love, and am happy that you are all well. God should bless you with long

life. We spent Pesach very pleasantly, even though, with my small children, it was hard to do without bread. Still, we were strictly careful with everything for the entire eight days. My five-year-old, may she live to 100, asked all Four Questions. Our nearly-four-year-old asked two questions,

Letter from Behr to his father in Lithuania, 1887, (from a set of letters held by the Jewish Theological Seminary).

you could see he was sleepy. My little Jacob sat at his father's side like a little man, only he had to keep shaking himself to stay awake, and he kept on babbling, and he drank, too. The baby, the tiny one, observed the whole ceremony, and it must have satisfied him, he behaved very well. We were very proud. Please write sometime in German or Yiddish so I can understand. My husband, God bless him, never finds the time to explain your letters to me.

From me, your daughter-in-law, Nesha Manischewitz
P.S. When I have more time, I'll write nicer.

She felt silly when she handed the letter back to Behr. In her exuberance, she had written out her married name in full. It was such a strong, important-sounding name.

Manischewitz!

She still had not found a good moment to ask him how he had chosen the name. Should she ask him now? She hesitated as she put away the writing materials, and then decided against it. *I suppose I like the mystery*, she thought. So the moment passed, and she never asked.

* * *

That summer, Behr and a friend named Moshe Isaacs got together and started to work on their project for the creation of a Jewish school. His own sons were hardly ready for it. But the project was symbolic. It meant they were on their way to taking charge of their own lives in America.

Behr and his friend made contact with Orthodox Jews from all of the city's congregations, and together they formed a committee of sixteen men. They called themselves the Cincinnati Talmud Torah Society, and each man made a small contribution. They received larger donations from a couple of German Jewish merchants, and hired two teachers. The men hoped to create an all-day school, but they began more modestly, with after-school classes. With only two teachers, there would be no class for the little girls. For the boys there would be four hours of classes, starting at four in the afternoon, after the children had been in public school all day.

Did Behr think everyone had as much energy as he did? Nesha was only taking care of the household and the four children, which was not too much for a woman of thirty, but somehow she was always exhausted at night.

Probably that meant she was pregnant again.

*　*　*

It was a crisp March morning in 1888. Behr paused in the doorway, on his way to work, and turned to speak to his wife, who stood stoutly behind him as she did every morning, waiting to close the door after him.

"I'm going to bake matzos this year, and sell them to our community, and maybe to others too. We'll see how it goes."

He said it with a half-smile, as though it wasn't so important to him whether it would go well or not. But Behr seldom made a casual remark.

She smiled back at him. "What a fine thing. With God's help!" And then he was gone.

Behr's announcement echoed pleasantly in her mind as she began her day's work.

Everybody needed matzos. But they had to be made precisely according to the religious prescriptions, and for this reason they were always baked under a rabbi's supervision, or even baked by the rabbi himself. It was a man's job. Nesha could bake bread and cakes and muffins and much more, but she would never dream of baking matzos. You had to bake them exactly the right amount of time, just eighteen minutes. Probably that was why it could not be left to women.

The baby might cry just when you wanted to take them out of the oven, and then they would be spoiled.

You had to take other special precautions too. You had to clean the oven in between batches till it was spotless. You couldn't re-use the little bits of dough that you'd trimmed off.

Behr would know exactly how to do it. He loved the Jewish laws and regulations. He loved machines, and he understood how an oven worked. Their oven at home was a secondhand one. Behr had taken it to a repair shop, where he'd watched and questioned every move the repairman made. When it broke down again, he'd fixed it himself.

The first oven that he used for the matzos was also second-hand. He got a good bargain on it, cleaned it, and modified it for matzo baking.

The sale of the matzos in the community went well. When the family sat down to the first holiday meal, Behr's matzos were on the table. He was beaming. For a few minutes, right at the holiday table, he was again the little boy who loved machines.

"This is it," he said. His excitement filled the air. "Next year, with God's help, I'll make twice as many matzos. I'll discuss it with Oscherowitz, so next time he'll be prepared in advance, when I start my baking."

He paused. Then he picked up the Passover holiday prayer book, the Haggadah.

"And now, no more talk of material things."

* * *

It was a pleasantly warm morning in the spring of 1892, and the sun streamed across the table. Henrietta's charitable group was gathered at her home, a modest frame house on Cutter Street. The women sat around a table with a big basket of clothing do-nated by wealthier women, and did the mending, chatting com-panionably as they worked. They talked about the poor Jews who would receive their aid.

"I watched an immigrant family arriving at the train station yesterday," said a plump, middle-aged woman named Fanny.

"They first caught my eye because the father was waiting alone with a handcart, all out of breath and lost-looking. He must have been at least fifty, the poor man, and he had a long, stringy beard and wore those strange black clothes and the hat with a peculiar brim."

She paused for breath, and one of the women asked,

"Were they Jewish?"

Fanny nodded: "I could tell he was one of those Lithuanian Jews, because I read about them in the *Israelite*. After a while the mother and the children climbed off the train, and the children were all raggedy and hungry looking, and you could see the little ones had been crying. The little girl was carrying a doll with its head broken off. My heart went out to them."

"Nesha's children had no playthings at all when they arrived," Henrietta said. "She said they were stolen on the boat."

At this, the women turned to Henrietta curiously, and someone asked, "Who is Nesha?"

Fanny, who was the informal leader of the group, replied before Henrietta could speak.

"Henrietta has actually befriended one of the new immigrant women, haven't you, Henny?"

She turned to Henrietta encouragingly. Henrietta was embarrassed; she didn't want to outshine the others.

"Well, I do what I can. They are so hard-working. Dov Behr Manischewitz is the husband's name," she added.

"An unusual name, isn't it?" someone asked.

Henrietta nodded. Someone else spoke up.

"My husband says that we only try to help the new immigrants because we are embarrassed for the Gentiles to see how queer and old-fashioned they look," the woman interjected.

"I don't think so," said Henrietta. "We help them because they're poor and they need our help. And because they're Jews."

"Well, yes, but it is embarrassing," admitted Fanny. "My Gentile neighbor asked me yesterday whether Jews are required to wear those funny hats, and I didn't know what to say."

Another friend broke in: "Why do they dress that way, Henrietta?"

Henrietta couldn't say. "Because they are pious, I suppose." She resolved to learn more about her odd little protégée on her next visit.

"How will their men ever get along, when they go looking for jobs in their long coats and beards, and funny black top hats?" asked Fanny. "Who will hire them?"

"And they don't even speak German, but only Yiddish," added another woman, "which is hard for an employer to understand."

"You needn't worry, at least not in this case," Henrietta replied. "Nesha's husband has started his own business already, baking and selling matzos for the Passover holiday. He started a couple of years ago and he is already doing very nicely. I promised her we would buy some this year."

"Matzos?" asked an American-born woman, looking so puzzled that Henrietta had to explain.

"Matzos are the unleavened bread that Jews are supposed to eat for a whole week during the Passover holiday, and not eat any bread at all. It is a way of remembering the time when the Jews were slaves to Pharaoh in Egypt. They left Egypt in a big hurry, so that the bread had no time to rise. On the first night of the holiday, one is supposed to recite the whole story of the exodus from Egypt, right at the Passover dinner table. The dinner even has a special name—the Seder. But I am afraid my husband and I have been very neglectful of this custom."

"We've been neglectful at my house too," said Fanny. "Because I didn't like to go to the Orthodox rabbi to buy the matzos. I was sure he would ask embarrassing questions about how we keep the holiday. And I would have to admit that I don't even buy kosher food!"

She paused. Then an idea came to her:

"But I'll be glad to buy some from your friend if you could order them for me, Henny."

"So will I, Henny," said the woman seated next to her. "It's a way of helping out."

By the time the conversation ended, Henrietta had received five or six orders for matzos from her friends. Even the woman who had professed ignorance of the custom said that she would buy some matzos—"so that the children will know we're Jewish," she said.

* * *

The lives of the assimilated Jewish woman named Henrietta and the pious young mother Nesha were already linked. So far, the relationship had been one-sided; Henrietta had been generous with her time and interest, and had helped Nesha over a few hard times. And right now, she had in her hand a list of orders for matzos that she taken from her friends, to help out by sending a little business to the young immigrant husband.

But when she thought about the matzos and her young religious friend Nesha, she had a queer thought that was new to her: Who was to say which way of living was the right one? Her own children had all but forgotten they were Jews. One of her daughters had already married a Protestant boy, much to Henrietta's shame, for such marriages were rare even among the most assimilated Jews. Her shame itself had been confused, since she was not religious and was baffled to discover that in her heart it mattered very much.

Recently her son Lee had bought his family a house on Mount Lookout in Cincinnati, overlooking the Ohio River. It was one of the new neighborhoods that had sprung up on the flat tops of the hills that surrounded the downtown river basin. New trolley cars went up to these neighborhoods, with curious cable-car arrangements in places where the hills were too steep for trolley cars.

No Jews lived there.

"All the way up there?" said Henrietta, when he told her about it.

"Don't you think your hard-working son deserves a house on a fancy hilltop?" Lee was perplexed by his mother's lack of joy in his success. He could afford the house. Didn't he own a first-class carriage business with a big sign over it saying "Lee Quitman Carriage and Livery Co."?

"I only meant, it's so far for your old mother to come visiting."

Lee's face cleared.

After her son left, Henrietta sat down to sort out her feelings. There was something she had learned about moving: the Jews always moved together. Even the assimilated Jews. At first the Jews had lived on the East End. And then, all in concert, they had moved over to the West End.

Now the Jews were moving to the hilltops. But again, though they were free to live everywhere, they had chosen just two neighborhoods, Walnut Hills and Avondale. None of them were moving to this place called Mount Lookout. Only her son Lee. And the thought preyed upon her mind.

"Do you find yourself thinking about religion more often lately?" she asked her friend Fanny. "Because of all the religious immigrants, I mean?" But her friend did not seem to be affected as Henrietta had been.

A few days later, Henrietta took her son by surprise. They were sitting together in his parlor, drinking tea.

"It's time you started doing a Passover dinner, a Seder, the way your father sometimes did it. Your children are old enough for it now."

Lee looked like he was about to agree, when he remembered something else.

"Can't read the Hebrew, Mama. Sorry."

But she had already thought of this. "One of the ladies in my group has a Passover book written completely in English. I'll bring it for you next week."

And so it was agreed.

On the day before Passover, Henrietta went to pick up her order of freshly baked matzos at the little bakery on Clarke Street that belonged to Nesha's husband, Behr Manischewitz.

An old woman wearing a big kerchief wrapped up the bundle of warm matzos and tied it securely with string. She handed it to Henrietta with a big smile and said something incomprehensible—probably wishing her a good holiday. Henrietta smiled back at her.

The next evening, a full moon shone on her son's big white house and the tall trees around it. A beam of light from the window fell on Henrietta as she emerged from the taxicab with her bundle of matzos.

The evening was a great success. Henrietta's son Lee loved his role of storyteller at the Passover table. His voice boomed out. "This is the bread of affliction, that our forefathers ate in the Land of Egypt." The children listened spellbound to the age-old story of the exodus from Egypt, which is always fresh and new, no matter how many times it is retold. They learned for the first time how the Red Sea had parted to let the fleeing Jews across. And how Pharaoh's army had followed them—on horses!—and how the sea had drowned them. "Amen!" shouted the children, when their father finished, and dug into the food. There was plenty of it, and the children polished off the matzos, enchanted by the novelty of the crispy disks.

Henrietta rode home in the carriage her son had summoned for her, deeply moved by the evening's success. She had brought a precious Jewish tradition back into her family's life. They would not forget their roots.

Chapter 3

With a Strong Hand

Israel saw the great hand that the Lord laid against
Egypt; and the people feared the Lord, and they believed
in the Lord and in His servant Moses.

Exodus 14:30–31

After Behr's first success with the matzos in 1888, Nesha thought
it was fair to expect an even better year in 1889. But that was not
what God had planned for her. When the year started she was
nearly nine months pregnant—again. She gave birth to another
daughter in January. She did not really mind having another girl.
After all, she was already the mother of three sons, and one more
daughter would be one more helper. No, it was just the tedium
and the hard work stretching out ahead that made the January
birth seem inauspicious.

She was not the only one who was finding that they had got-
ten off to a less than perfect start. Behr took the birth of another
daughter almost as an affront. He had quite simply expected a
fourth son, though admittedly he could cite no law of nature or
Talmud to justify his expectation. His frustration mingled with
anger at himself for his foolish assumption. And so this daughter
received none of the welcome given the first daughter. With
hardly any deliberation, Behr chose the name Rose, which was
both an Old World name and an American one. After the naming he paid no more attention to her. Nesha was left with an end-

less prospect of hard work. What had she expected? Her dreams of the good life in America were stored in the ice-box.

As if God wanted to remind them that life was not to be taken for granted, sickness followed the birth. Before the winter was past, all of the children got the measles, one after another. In March Behr somehow did the matzo baking, and managed to get the matzos to all of last year's customers and to some new ones. But coming home each night to a house full of sickness took a toll on him. Before the measles were completely gone, Behr was sick too, with a fever and cough. Then one of the little ones caught pneumonia, which was frightening and required several expensive visits from a doctor. The sound of coughing was still heard in the house for weeks after the sickness had passed.

Somehow Nesha remained well enough to take care of them all and to breastfeed the new baby. It was hard, lonesome work. Where were her new friends? In June, she told Behr how she felt. Not that she expected him to understand, but she had hardly left the house in months, and she had to tell someone. She was nearly in tears.

"Not to speak evil, but I do think the rebbetzin or the other women could have come to see if I need some help. Or just to talk. Like at home." She sniffled. "Nobody came at all but the charity woman, Henrietta. None of our own people."

Nesha was careful not to say more. Behr did not know how much the charity woman had helped her. Henrietta always came in the daytime, in his absence.

"No wonder you're disappointed," Behr said, shaking his head in sympathy. "Here in America nobody helps like they do at home. Everybody is busy with himself."

Nesha stared at Behr, startled that to see that he understood her feelings.

"But our friends here are the same people as the people at home," she protested.

Behr shook his head. "In America they breathe different air."

"Well, it shouldn't change what's in their hearts," Nesha said, wondering if it was true about the air. Her own children had changed already, they were freer and wilder. She was sure Behr hadn't noticed it yet, and she certainly was not going to be the first to tell him. The air felt different here, heavier, and it lacked the sea breezes she remembered from home.

By the time the whole family was healthy again, the year had ended. Behr had done all right with the matzo sales, in spite of all the illness, but the year was something of a setback. Behr did not even write to his father until the next January, and he did not mention his new business in the letter.

The following year, 1890, was a good year for business. Behr opened a second tiny bakery, not far from the first. This year also began with another baby, in February, a boy this time, to Behr's delight. Mordechai was the name he chose for the baby—a weighty name for an infant.

Behr smiled at the baby at Nesha's side, looking more relaxed than he had been since before last year's illness. He fondled the tiny hands.

"Mordechai?" Nesha said softly, trying out the sound of it.

"Max in English," Behr informed her. "The two names sound well together." Nesha stared at him. So her little deception with Mayme about the name had really paid off. Behr had got used to the idea of using American names.

He smiled broadly as he cleared his throat for the informal new-baby blessing that had become his habit.

"Another son, may he live a long life of success, learning, and *mitzvos*, and to help me in my matzo business, God willing."

Nesha beamed back at him. The change in Behr's blessing amused her. She tried to imagine a house full of grown sons, all in baker's aprons. Right now, it was a house full of dirty laundry! She would have to get back on her feet quickly.

As always when a boy was born into the family, Behr was in good humor that lasted for weeks. He came back to Nesha's bed as soon as she was pure again and made the required visit to the *mikvah.* She didn't mind his haste, for she was happy to see him in such good spirits. But the mound of laundry still weighed on her mind even as he lay with her.

The next year, 1891, should have been another good one because Behr had added another bakery to the first two locations, and hired two new workers to run it. But it was all spoiled by a controversy that arose in the community.

Was the controversy only about Behr and his matzos, or was something else behind it?

Nesha and the other women never found out for sure. Maybe it was just about power, as men's struggles often seemed to be. There was a rabbi in each camp, and the men were divided about equally behind them. Each group was equally pious. This was odd, because piety was so important to the men; if it had been about who was more pious, that would have made some sense. But no. In fact, the scholars from both groups went to the same house of study together. Probably now they were sitting there on the benches like so many quarreling schoolboys, with each group elbowing the other out of the way to take the best places.

But it was no joke, because Behr's living, his *parnossah,* was at stake. The rabbi of the opposing camp sold his own matzos and sent notices all over town advertising them. He did it just to harm Behr, for he had little to gain financially from the sales. Behr had some strong supporters, but some enemies too. His well-known piety was no defense.

There was a lot of maneuvering and rumor-mongering. It took until March for the rumors to reach Nesha. She ignored them for several anxious days. Then she decided to speak, after dinner when her husband was most approachable.

"Behr, I'm worried about something." She hesitated. "One of the women said maybe it isn't allowed to use machinery to make matzos."

Behr looked at her so gravely that she was astonished. Did the women's gossip matter so much? But of course it did matter. The legitimacy of the matzo product was the basis of everything. It was so crucial that even the women must be convinced.

"That question was first raised nearly forty years ago already, when machinery was new," he told her. He spoke slowly, the way he spoke to his small sons when he wanted to be sure they understood every word.

"The pious Jews in New York wrote to rabbis in Europe: to the *posek*, the interpreter of laws, Rabbi Joseph Saul Nathanson, and then to the rabbis of Cracow and Danzig, and also to the rabbi of Gleiwitz in Prussia, a wise man and a talmudic scholar, may the memory of the righteous be blessed."

He repeated the whole list of names a second time before continuing.

"All those learned rabbis made it clear that machine-made matzos are perfectly acceptable."

"The rabbi of Gleiwitz's reply was published in the New York newspaper, the *Asmonean*, in February, 1851." A yellowed copy of that very precious article was locked in his desk at the matzo bakery. Plenty of rabbis had objected too. Should he tell his wife? The objectors were also important rabbis: Rabbi Solomon Kluger of Brody, Rabbi Solomon Halberstam of Sanz, and the Gerer Rebbe.

No, he decided, it wasn't necessary. His wife only needed to be reassured that he had religious authority to support him—which he did.

"The rabbis here in Cincinnati know about this decision. They are deliberately allowing false rumors to spread," he said. He hesitated before continuing. "Besides, strictly kosher matzos are already being produced in at least one factory. I'm not the first to do it."

He waited for her reaction to this new information, but she only nodded. She did not care whether he was the first. That was a man's concern—being first. She only wanted things to go well for her husband.

"In Philadelphia a man named Goodman, a German Jew, but pious, has been baking them ever since the Civil War ended, over thirty years now."

"I am glad it's a rumor, and not, God forbid, the truth," said Nesha.

She would sleep better tonight. Not only because her husband was backed by important rabbis but because he had omitted to ask her who was spreading the rumor. The Evil Tongue, the spreading of rumors, was a serious sin, and she was afraid that even repeating the rumor to her husband might also be forbidden.

Apparently it was not, for the next morning Behr went immediately to the rabbi's study to discuss her report on the women's gossip. He remained there for hours. When he returned home he went directly into the kitchen where Nesha was making noodles. Without looking at her directly, he announced, "The rabbi has written to six distinguished rabbis in Lithuania so that they can intervene against these fools." He turned around before she could reply and left the kitchen as quickly as he entered it.

The same evening, Behr wrote to his father in Lithuania, asking him to intercede. From the moment he mailed the letter, Behr's agitation increased. In the evenings he returned from work with scarcely a word for anyone. He sat down at his desk for a scant five minutes, then reappeared in the hallway, hat in hand. "I've a meeting with the rabbi," he said, and disappeared out the door. He might return for dinner, or only late in the night. Twice daily he waited for the mailman, with narrowed eyes and fingers tapping on his desk. At last his father's letter arrived. Behr snatched it from the postman and ran indecorously into his home office to read it, not bothering to close the door.

It was a long letter filled with philosophical thoughts:

You should only avoid controversy for the rest of your life, because peace is the source of all the goodness of the world, and likewise, opposing it, controversy causes the world to lose all its goodness. This is what we read in the writings of Maimonides: do not defile your souls with controversy, which destroys the body, the soul and livelihood. . . . Therefore, my son, I command you, do not enter into any quarrel, whether in connection with the city's business, or its organizations. And even if it seems to you that the quarrel is for the sake of heaven, do not let your inclination tempt you.

Nesha peered around the half-open door and watched as he read the letter twice, then a third time, clenching it so hard that his knuckles whitened. Obviously it wasn't what he'd wanted to hear. He thrust the letter into his desk drawer and slammed the drawer shut.

Before her anxious eyes, he stormed out of the house. She did not try to read the letter, much as she knew it was going to affect her own life. Reading someone else's letters was probably a sin; she wasn't sure. Anyway she would learn soon enough what the results were.

Behr strode through the city to clear his mind, instinctively avoiding the streets where he was likely to meet any friends. He headed along the downtown canal and north toward the open-air Findlay Market and the narrow streets of the non-Jewish German neighborhood, the one they called Over-the-Rhine. The atmosphere there was not so different from the Friedrich's market back in Memel, and the familiarity of it calmed him. His life nowadays was a daily struggle in a foreign place; never was he so aware of this as when he left it behind him momentarily, to walk on a street where the familiar sounds of German echoed from the market stalls.

His father was right: the controversy had been eating at his soul. *Read between the lines*, he admonished himself: his father was not telling him to give up his enterprise, but rather, to find another way to reach his objective, without contention. The rabbinical concept of *masig g'vul*, or unfair competition, an important element of rabbinical law that he and his rabbi had been planning to see enforced against their enemies—what good would come of it? He needed good will, not enemies. He would quite simply make the best matzo and find the most efficient way of producing it. The other rabbi would know when he was beaten.

When he returned home, he greeted his wife more pleasantly than he had done in weeks. Nesha watched him closely for the next few days, until she was sure that the storm had passed its apogee. Soon there were no more letters, and fewer private conversations with the rabbi. Life went on, the holiday came and went, and the Passover dishes were returned to their trunk for another year. The controversy slowly receded, as such things do.

Nesha gave birth to another son that year, just thirteen months after the previous birth. This one was a quiet, peaceful baby, with smooth, brown hair and big round eyes that reminded her of a deer, which was the meaning of the Jewish name that they gave him: Hirsh.

Behr blessed him as always, but there was a tiredness in his blessing. His energy was still focused on the aftermath of the controversy and its effects on his business. *Next year*, he was thinking, *I'll need a new strategy.*

His routine was necessarily disturbed somewhat during the week after the birth, when his wife was not exactly "lying in" but still limited in carrying out her chores. The first week with a new baby boy was a special time for the father, who made arrangements for the circumcision ceremony to be held on the eighth day, and in general made himself helpful in dealing with errands, while his wife remained at home for her brief respite. All too soon for Nesha, the day of the ceremony arrived, requiring her to return to full-scale preparation of food.

By the first work day of the baby's second week, Behr was behaving as if everything were normal again. In the morning he accepted the freshly ironed shirt that his wife handed him as his due. He swallowed his tea distractedly, aloof from the commotion around him as the older children prepared to leave for school. With scarcely more than a nod of his head, he went out the door to begin his work day.

In the relative quiet that followed, Nesha allowed herself a long sigh and turned to look at the small apartment that was her entire world.

The younger children chattered softly in their bed and the baby was beginning to stir. It was going to be another day amidst mounds of dishes and soiled baby garments and the cooking that had to be done all by her own hand, kneading bread and slicing noodles and scrubbing the floor and mending clothing while the food was in the oven.

She hardly expected help from her husband. *Parnossah*, livelihood, was a man's first duty, just as important as Torah study, which, God forgive the comparison, was also a man's duty, if he was capable of it. But she was thirty-four and had been pregnant every year for the past ten years. Couldn't he at least notice that she, too, was working hard? The daily tasks came easily to her now, and she never got any special consideration from Behr after childbirth. She had done a good job of accepting her lot as a woman, hadn't she?

A man is allowed, and even encouraged, to refrain from coming to his wife in her bed for a while after childbirth, if he sees she needs a rest. The rebbetzin herself had said this recently to the women in the congregation. Nesha's jaw dropped when she heard this piece of news. She had thought that the law to "be fruitful and multiply" required a man to keep on coming to his wife all the time, except during her monthly period and the seven days that followed it, and the similarly brief waiting period that followed childbirth. It was beginning to anger her to realize that Behr, who must know about the leniency the rebbetzin had spoken of, behaved as if he did not.

Even Behr's brother in Telz—a pious man if ever there was one, so pious he did not even think of moving with his family to the impious New World—even he did not have such a big family. Just one son, a boy named Jacob like her own precious son, and a daughter or two. She was not quite sure about the daughters because Behr no longer wrote letters to the Old Country as often as he used to.

Sure enough, the next year Nesha was pregnant again. A baby girl was born in November 1892. They called this one Rachel; Rae would be her English name. Nesha was thirty-five now, with eight living children. Five sons, three daughters—so many blessings, so much exhaustion.

As she lay in bed with the new baby girl, she stared at the ceiling and worked out a plan. From now on, she would mentally resist her husband's seed each time he came to her in bed. If she concentrated very hard on this, could that make the pregnancies stop? She didn't ask anyone, because she was embarrassed. But this time she didn't rush to the *mikvah* so soon after the birth; she deliberately waited an extra week. And when Behr finally came to her, she closed her eyes and resisted.

Maybe her method worked, because after that year there were no more babies. Miscarriages—several of them—but no babies. When the births stopped, there was a subtle change in the pulse of the family's life. It was now paced by the matzo bakery.

Each spring, before the Passover holiday, Nesha bought new dresses for her daughters, and even a new dress for herself, with Behr's permission (hoping she was right about the pregnancies). She began to enjoy the life of a well-to-do baker's wife. With a nice new coat, and her little girls in frilly dresses, things appeared at last to be going just as she had imagined under the marriage canopy.

Each year, Behr began making matzos earlier in the season. He announced his baking calendar on the first of January, after dinner.

"We'll start in February this year." As he spoke, Nesha paused in putting away the last items from the table.

"God willing," she said. "But will they stay fresh so long?"

Behr actually laughed at this. "I tested it already."

He had brought home some matzos one day last summer, and the children had exclaimed in joy over the out-of-season treat. "Is it allowed?" the oldest boy, Meyer, had asked, and Behr had beamed with pride over his son's question. "Yes, it is allowed to eat matzos any time," he explained, "except during the last month before the holiday, in order to make the special blessing upon eating them the first time." Nesha had been surprised at her husband's playfulness—matzos in summer!—and then she had forgotten about it.

"So they will stay fresh, said Nesha, smiling. "A blessing."

Then Behr turned serious. "The controversy in the community served one purpose," he said. "It showed me that I must sell matzos outside of Cincinnati." This was the strategy he had planned over the year.

Nesha folded the dinner napkins as she considered this new idea. "The Jews in small towns need matzos too," she said.

All though January and February, before the baking got into full swing, Behr traveled to the Jewish communities in the surrounding cities and towns. He visited the rabbis, prayed in the synagogues, and spoke with the grocers. As soon as the leaders of a community met Behr, and saw his Orthodoxy and sincerity, they were won over. They would buy his matzos at the local grocery store, and the local rabbi would not need to bake his own matzos anymore.

By the next year Behr needed more workers than he could easily find among the religious men of the community. He mulled over this for a while, and he even told Nesha his worry.

"I don't want to attract men away from the cigar factory," he said. The cigar factory was owned by a religious Jew, who shut it down for all the Jewish holidays. For this reason it was a popular place of employment for recent immigrants who were religious Jews.

"Why not?" said Nesha. "The factory jobs don't pay so well."

"But I need workers for only two or three months. Suppose after the holiday the cigar maker won't take them back, and then I have, God forbid, taken away a man's livelihood."

He frowned. "I don't want another controversy, and you know, even if he takes them back, it might not look so good."

"You'll think of something."

* * *

A couple of days after the start of the matzo-baking season, Nesha received a visit from the rebbetzin. As soon as her coat was off, she said, "So, you know what the old women are doing this year for their holiday money?"

Nesha paused with the rebbetzin's coat still in her hands. "Old women?"

"They're working for your husband, God send long life to him!"

The rebbetzin's big smile showed how pleased she was to be the first with the news. "You know why it's always men who make matzos?"

She didn't wait for an answer. "It's only because if the woman has her period, and hasn't been to the *mikvah*, she shouldn't touch holy things. The older women, God bless them, don't need the *mikvah* anymore, they are pure as babies!"

The old women were good, careful workers, year after year. And there was no more controversy in the community.

* * *

After the recruitment of the old women, the growth of the bakery settled into a pattern. Behr's confidence grew as he built upon what he had learned: avoiding conflict, promoting business through personal contact, and knowing his machinery.

He spoke less of his work at home now, as though life were more easily broken into neat compartments now that the anxiety over their survival was gone. It should have been the best time of all for Nesha, with no more pregnancies and a big healthy family to be proud of. But something in Behr would not allow her this pleasure.

It irked him enormously that his brother's son Jacob in Telz was receiving the kind of religious education that his own sons in America would never receive. The letters from the Old Country had become a reproach, no longer a pleasure. It rankled whenever Behr's father passed on a letter. To save paper the letters made a three-way-trip: from father in the village to his elder son in Telz, then to the second son in America. The father always inquired in his letters about the progress the boy Jacob in Telz was making in his studies. The same letters passed in silence over the education of Behr's sons in the heathen wasteland of America.

Behr tore up more than one of these letters, nearly suffocating with shame and frustration.

And he became stern and unforgiving with his sons, like the harshest teachers at the yeshivas in the Old Country.

He managed to impose his will on them on the weekend, when they were under his command without respite. But school days were fraught with danger. A boy would misbehave, and Behr would hear about it. Nesha feared Mondays most of all. The boys' pent-up energy was released at the end of the school day, in the Talmud Torah.

She ran out of her kitchen at eight one Monday evening, hearing Meyer's yelp of pain. Behr was gripping the boy's arm. His fierce voice drowned out the boy's scream.

"What is this the teacher tells me about tar-baby?"

Meyer grinned at his father's mispronunciation of the unfamiliar word. It was a fatal mistake. Behr slapped the boy's face. "Did you put this thing, this tar-baby on your teacher's chair?" The boy's grin twisted into a frightened grimace. "Yes, Papa."

He received a beating that he would not soon forget. The father stopped only when the boy was blubbering helplessly, his grin forgotten.

"Behr, don't hurt him," Nesha said boldly, but it was too late, for he had already finished.

He turned to Joseph, who was cringing in a corner. The younger boy's whole body trembled violently when his father pulled him out of his hiding place. "You were in this mischief, too, weren't you?" Behr said in a fearsome voice. But even as he spoke, his anger seemed to fade. Joseph whimpered as though he had already been beaten, which made the beating useless. A few halfhearted blows were all the frustrated father could muster.

After the beating, Behr stood up straight and turned calmly to Nesha, as though the incident had never happened. "If my clean shirt is laid out," he said with icy dignity, (it was always laid out), "I will be ready for dinner shortly."

Shaken, Nesha nodded. The two boys slunk away to their room. She dared not follow them to wash their tear-stained faces or show any other sign of sympathy. Hugs and sympathy were not a part of this family's life anyway, even in quieter moments.

So she returned to her kitchen. There she discovered her second son, Jacob, sitting on a stool, waiting.

"My dear one," she said, moderating her voice so as not to be heard outside the kitchen. Jacob's face brightened into a smile. He was used to such terms of endearment when they were alone. And he'd already figured out that he was mama's favorite. "Yes, Mama?"

"You weren't with your brothers when they made this, this tear-baby?" She had no idea what the word meant.

"No, Mama, I was at the candy store." His wide smile beamed at her like sunlight on an overcast day.

Nesha picked up her apron from the counter and tied it around her waist. She felt in the pocket and pulled out a pineapple candy. It was a ritual, their private ritual.

"Oh, my favorite candy, where did this come from?" She looked around the room as if another little boy might be hiding there. Jacob beamed with pleasure.

For a moment Nesha forgot the scene in the hall. She knew in a flash that she loved her son Jacob more than anyone in the world. More than the harsh, stiff-necked man who fumed in the hall, furiously straightening his collar for dinner.

Dinner was soon on the table. But the tasty, nourishing food might as well have been ashes, for all the pleasure it brought.

The father's face was as stiff and ugly as the stone idols in a Bible story. Nesha spoke as little as possible, though she wanted very much to know about the tear-baby and whether it was really such a serious offense. The punished boys were silent. Though innocent, Jacob wisely remained silent too.

The younger children whined and fidgeted, feeling the tension in the air. Behr ignored them, as he always did. Until they were old enough to learn Torah, they were of no interest to him.

He was, after all, merely following the example of his own father, a model of piety. The sullen faces at the table only showed him how necessary it was to be severe.

Nesha was angry with Behr all through the evening. She gave no outward sign of it, but before she closed the shutters, she spoke her thoughts silently to the night sky.

How dare you make my sons' lives so bitter when they are just young boys? How can you be so educated and yet not see that you are not in Telz anymore? These boys are American boys, and they sit in Talmud Torah so many long hours while their irreligious friends are playing baseball. They do their lessons mostly, and they say their prayers mostly, but it's never enough for you.

You're teaching them another lesson. You're teaching them that piety is a matter of coercion and punishment. They'll hate our beautiful religion when you are finished, and even so you won't keep them from breathing the free air of America.

In the morning, her anger had settled into resentment. The boys were clever like their father, she thought grimly. They would find a way to live with him.

Meyer soon became skillful at lying to his father. This gave him some freedom. It also put a permanently sneaky expression on his face.

Jacob would never resort to lying. When his father accused him of a misdemeanor, the boy's angry eyes flashed right back at him. At first, he too got his share of beatings. But he soon found his salvation in two places.

The first place was the schoolyard. He played ball passionately until his energy was totally spent, and he returned home so exhausted that no fatherly provocation could get much of a reaction from him. The second place where he found a safe harbor was under his mother's protective wing. There was no way she could defend him in his father's presence. But in her kitchen, he was a cherished prince, his mama's boy, the precious baby she'd nearly lost.

The third son, Joseph, learned to shrink into the woodwork, sliding through the house toward the door, entering and leaving like a cautious scout advancing through a forest of wild animals.

The girls never came under such close scrutiny and were in this way freer. The eldest, Mayme, was a big help to Nesha in the home, and her father noted this with approval. The girl spoke too loud and too often. Had she learned this in the schoolyard? "A girl should always speak softly," Nesha admonished her over and over, with no success. But in every other way she was compliant—and safe from her father's anger.

Behr's harshness, anger, and punishments spoiled these years for Nesha, which should have been the best years of all.

She pitied the younger children who still thought that their father could be pleased if they washed their hands obediently and said a blessing. They had yet to discover that his demand for compliance was insatiable. She never allowed herself to become too close to the little ones, so as not to be hurt when they made this discovery in their turn.

Even so the little ones were a pleasure to her, especially in the daytime, while Behr was at work. Max was a thoroughly boyish little boy with perpetually dirty knees, and pockets bulging with marbles and other treasures he won from his playmates. Little Hirsh had big eyes and endless curiosity, was quick to cry and just as quick to laugh, often at the same time. Shy little Rose went mostly unnoticed. She usually played at the neighbor's house until dinnertime and then slipped quietly into her seat at the table. The baby, Rae, was sweet and docile, a plaything to the others.

* * *

In the last years of the nineteenth century, each of the older boys in turn approached his thirteenth year, the year of his religious maturity. Tension mounted before each Bar Mitzvah. Would the boy meet his father's expectations?

The first Bar Mitzvah was in 1897. Nesha breathed a sigh of relief when Meyer carried out his performance without a hitch. "No more Talmud Torah for me," he gloated to his envious brothers right after the ceremony. Behr overheard him, and the atmosphere at dinner was frigid. Once the children had gone to their rooms, the father let out his scorn to Nesha's ears only.

"Our eldest son has the mind of a peasant," he hissed.

Behr had received a letter from Telz that Friday afternoon, on the eve of the Bar Mitzvah. The letter informed him that his brother's son Jacob was doing well in his Talmud studies. "We are proud, though we keep this from him so he may grow in modesty as well as in learning," wrote Behr's brother. "We hope to keep him at his books another year, though he is a strong lad and his mother sorely needs his help at the cafe." Behr had torn up the letter—before the Sabbath, when tearing was forbidden— to ease his anger, but still it rankled. His own second son Jacob was bright, brighter than Meyer—surely as bright as that boy

Jacob in Telz—but he was an indifferent student, at public school as well as at the Talmud Torah.

In the stifling Cincinnati summer of 1898, Jacob turned thirteen. "I want you all to call me Jake now," he announced to his family on the morning of his Bar Mitzvah, proud to be old enough to assert himself in this way. On this day, even his father had to nod his agreement.

Jacob/Jake performed the Bar Mitzvah ceremony impeccably. He stood straight and tall, his blue eyes shining. He wore his first suit, made for him by Behr's skillful tailor, a pious man who dressed all the wealthier Jewish men, or at least all those who cared about their appearance but cared, too, about the law of *shatnes*. This law forbade the mixing of different kinds of cloth—a restriction only the more pious men even knew about.

Behr made a formal speech in honor of his son at the Sabbath table, as a father should do on his second son's Bar Mitzvah.

But something was missing from Behr's satisfaction. Nesha saw it, and was uneasy. *He wants something more of Jake.* What would it be?

Jake could grasp a complex argument and find the fault in it quickly, in the same way that his father could. With his quick mind, Jake had unwittingly let his father know that he was capable of learning Talmud if he would only turn his mind in that direction.

* * *

It was a quiet Sabbath day early in the third month of the new century. The noon meal had been eaten, the end-of-meal blessing recited, and the older children had disappeared to their rooms. Nesha was tranquilly clearing the last dishes from the table.

Behr leaned forward in his chair and spoke quietly. "I've decided to send our son Jake to Jerusalem to study."

Nesha dropped the bowl she was carrying. It fell back onto the table with a hollow thud.

Behr continued. "Jake has the mind of a scholar, if only he can be forced to use it. Only such a strong measure will do the job." His voice told her that his decision was already final.

She sat down heavily in the nearest chair. Thoughts raced through her mind. Her favorite son. She loved him as he was. Bright, naughty, generous, disobedient. Clever with his hands. Or at memorizing a poem. Or at tinkering with machinery like his father. Was he at risk of becoming a non-believer? Was this the only way to protect him? By sending him off to a place where even his life wouldn't be safe?

"The Holy Land is under the rule of the Turks, worse than the tsar of Russia," she said aloud, still stunned, not quite believing this was happening. A dusty, half-abandoned land. There were anti-Jewish riots, food and water shortages, and the climate was harsh. And it was not the only place a boy could study. Of course it was not the only place. How could Behr fail to see the obvious?

"You could at least send him back to Europe," she cried out. "He could study in Telz, for God's sake. He would be with your brother there and not among strangers!" She felt her voice rise to a shriek, and didn't care.

Her husband had planned it all, she realized now. The letters from Europe had become less frequent. And there had been letters bearing the strange Turkish postmark of the Holy Land. Names of rabbis in the Holy Land were on Behr's lips often lately, and the familiar Old Country names seemed not to count for much any more. Palestine, yes, it was all very well to support the pious rabbis who lived in the Holy Land amidst dust and poverty. But to drag her own precious son into this new mania of his?

Behr continued, unperturbed by his wife's outburst.

"And we'll be sending Max along too," he said. Max was just ten years old. "Joseph is preparing for his Bar Mitzvah," he added, as though this explained anything. "Max is a better choice."

"A better choice. A ten-year-old." Nesha's voice dripped sarcasm. "And how long will you make them stay there? Until they are nineteen?"

Then she realized in horror that this was exactly what he meant. *That was how long the studies were back in Telz.* "They will be strangers to us when they return!" She shrieked the words.

Behr's voice came back at her as quick and loud as thunder. "They will be God-fearing men when they return!"

Behr rose abruptly and left the room, leaving the echo of his words.

Somehow Nesha got through that Sabbath. An icy March rain beat down on the house, and the curtains hung darkly over the bay windows, matching the bleakness in her heart. Dusk fell long before Behr performed the Havdalah ceremony that marked the Sabbath's end.

Behr waited until just after Passover to inform his two sons. He summoned them into his home office and closed the door. They emerged half an hour later and went to their rooms. Jake looked sullen, but not the younger boy. A train ride, an ocean voyage, an adventure—what did a ten-year-old understand?

Behr had chosen a yeshiva and a reliable Jerusalem family for the boys to board with. He had arranged this through contacts and correspondence.

A couple of emissaries from Jerusalem were expected in Cincinnati at the beginning of May. Their task was to collect money from pious Jews to support the yeshivas and other institutions in the Holy City. Cincinnati was their last stop. Behr had arranged for them to stay over the Sabbath and then remain for two more nights. They would depart by train on the following Monday morning, taking Jake and Max with them on the journey back to Jerusalem.

Nesha packed the boys' clothes blindly, not even asking Jake which things he wanted to take. What did it matter? He would open the trunk far away in Jerusalem, lost to her forever.

On Friday night the two emissaries came to dinner. They stood with the family while Behr pronounced the Sabbath evening *Kiddush*, the blessing over the wine. Jake was seated opposite them.

Nesha saw her son silently taking in every detail of the strange men's appearance. She was so deep in sorrow that she would not have noticed the visitors' appearance at all, except that she was trying to see them through her son's eyes. The men had disheveled beards and long black coats that hung unevenly.

Seated at the head of the table, Behr was sleek and well groomed, in striking contrast to his visitors. His Sabbath coat, traditional in cut, was well fitted and made of the best material. His white shirt was starched, and his beard was neatly trimmed and combed.

Like his father, Jake was neatly dressed. Despite the turmoil he must be going through, he had changed his shirt for the Sabbath meal, smoothed down his hair, and brushed his dark pants. How easy it was for the son to imitate his father's example when no punishment was involved!

The meal was very quiet. The only conversation was between Behr and the emissaries.

Jake disappeared to his room as soon as the final benediction was pronounced. For the rest of the Sabbath, he emerged only at mealtimes.

On Sunday, he was nowhere to be found.

"Jake?"

"Where is Jake?" The words echoed through the house all through the day, more anxiously at each missed meal. At dinnertime Behr stood at the front door, looking for once in his life helpless and confused.

"Has he, God forbid, had an accident?" He looked at Nesha.

Nesha's heart beat loudly as she realized the truth: her son had run away. Silently she prayed, *Run faster, my dear boy*.

What she said was: "God forbid! He may have only gone across town and lost his trolley fare!"

The house was lit up until midnight. Behr's anxiety alternated with anger, while Nesha went from window to door to window in agitation, with no thought of sleep.

The emissaries arrived at mid-morning. They could not wait more than a few hours; they would miss their train to New York. By this time, Behr had to face the realization that his son had run away.

The big trunk was standing in the hall, and ten-year-old Max was standing alongside it, looking sullen. In fact, he was terrified. He had not minded being sent to Jerusalem, or even to China, as long as his older brother was being sent with him. Now it looked as if he was going to be sent alone with the two strange men, who spoke no English, to a strange and foreign country, about which his brother Jake had told him quite a few frightening things.

Nesha stayed in the kitchen with Mayme, making as little noise as possible. The two younger children, Hirsh and Rose, hung in the doorway, watching their father silently.

Behr stood like a statue in the hall for a few moments. The emissaries waited for his instructions. At last he spoke.

"My son Jake will not be going with you," he said in Hebrew. His voice sounded very dignified. "We will be making a change of plans."

His gaze fell on the two little ones in the doorway. Eight-year-old Hirsh was looking at him wide-eyed. Behr turned back to address the emissaries.

"My son Hirsh will accompany his brother to Palestine. Please sit down, my daughter will make tea for you. My wife will need some time to pack my son's things, and I must prepare the documents."

Nesha dropped a pot on the floor with a loud clatter.

A small slip of an eight-year-old boy, to be sent off to the Holy Land? She quickly recovered herself. It would not do for the children to see that she was as horrified as they were. Especially for the little one who had now been chosen for the journey.

"Come, Hirsh," she said in a voice that she hoped was not shaking, "you must help me to select your clothes from the big clothes basket. Otherwise I might make a mistake." *And if I let you out of my sight, you might run away too.*

But little Hirsh obediently followed his mother to help her pack his clothes.

Nesha pulled all of Jake's clothes out of the big trunk, tossing them carelessly on his bed. She was embarrassed at the relief and elation she felt as she did this. A joyous image went through her mind: Jake would come back tomorrow, or the next day, and find the heap of clothes on his bed, and stuff them in the clothes basket, and be here as always, not on his way to Jerusalem.

Hirsh was leaning against the bedpost, watching her intently.

"Can I take Joseph's mittens, Mama?" The little voice sounded wistful. "Mine got lost."

She reached into the cupboard, pulled out the coveted mittens, and looked at them. They spoke of winter recess time in the schoolyard, snowball fights, sliding on ice. Last winter, little Hirsh had tried earnestly to explain to her about recess. He had invented a word for it in Yiddish, so she would understand: "Recess-*tzeit*, Mama, when we play in the snow." Were mittens needed in the Holy Land? Was there snow?

"You can take them, yes." The boy smiled at this small victory.

The older brother would forget about the mittens by the time winter came again to Cincinnati. By that time little Hirsh would be absorbed by his new life on the other side of the world. What would he become?

Ten-year-old Max was his own person already. But the younger boy's character was more volatile, as yet unformed. The English name given to him for his barely started public school career would be forgotten. He would keep the name Hirsh, and he would change utterly.

Somehow Nesha finished packing and managed to say a few encouraging words to the two boys who were about to leave. The two emissaries had finished their tea, and were standing a little impatiently in the hall.

The family stood motionless while Behr gave a parting lecture to the two boys. Nobody would remember a word of it.

When he finished, the two boys, framed on either side by the two emissaries, left the house.

That evening the house was silent. Behr disappeared into his home office, where he worked behind a closed door until bedtime.

Nesha stood for a long time at the rear window, looking out over the dark alleyway lined with ghostly work sheds, chicken coops, and the outdoor toilets of less affluent families. Was her boy looking up at the house from below? Was he watching their movements, gauging his father's fury? No. A boy of fourteen would have friends who would connive with him, hide him in their homes. He would not have to sleep in an alley or in a dark shed. After a long while she closed the curtain and went upstairs to her bed.

How had her life gone so wrong? Her favorite son was a fugitive. Her sweet, big-eyed eight-year-old was spending a fearful, sleepless night in a strange railroad car half-way to New York with two bearded strangers. Her self-reliant little ten-year-old, his pockets full of a boy's weaponry, was bouncing along in the train too, terrified but not showing it. And the remaining children at home were cowering under their covers, trembling for their own safety from their father's wrath. Maybe they were praying now for God's help, as she was, on this long night.

Chapter 4

Gathering Manna

*And the whole congregation of the children of Israel mur-
mured against Moses and against Aaron in the wilderness; and the children of Israel said unto them: "Would
that we had died by the hand of the Lord in the land of
Egypt, when we sat by the flesh-pots, when we did eat
bread to the full; for ye have brought us forth into this
wilderness, to kill this whole assembly with hunger."
Then said the Lord unto Moses: "Behold, I will cause to
rain bread from heaven for you; and the people shall go
out and gather a day's portion every day."*

—Exodus 16:2–4

Jake came back two days later, looking contrite. "You've done a
wicked thing and you'll be punished for it!" Behr threatened, but
his anger had a false ring. To Jake's surprise there was no beating.
"You're confined to your room for two months," Behr growled,
and an astonished Jake meekly answered, "Yes, Papa." It was a
harsh punishment for a boy whose life was mainly outside his
home, but Jake had won the battle.

When Nesha came in to make his bed, she discovered under
it a new stack of well-worn pocket novels. "I wonder where did
these come from," she said, hiding a smile.

"From Max," he said to her in a low, conspiratorial tone. And
so she knew what she had already guessed: he had spent the two
days in hiding at the home of his best friend, a boy named Max.

Behr wrote to Jerusalem and asked the boys' guardians to send him a photograph as proof that the boys had arrived safely and well. The photograph arrived after a few months. It showed the two boys standing stiffly in the striped silk robes that were the holiday garb of religious Jews in Jerusalem.

Behr placed it in a frame on the desk in his study, where Nesha—and sometimes the children—came in to look at it when Behr was not at home. And gradually the strange-looking boys in Jerusalem slipped further away, till they became as distant in their brothers' and sisters' thoughts as the Holy Land itself.

Hirsh and Max Manischewitz in Jerusalem (1900).

By sending two sons to Jerusalem, Behr had ensured the religious future of the family. With this load off his mind, he soon stopped lashing out at his remaining sons' impiety.

Mayme was her mother's good helpmate, even though she was still too outspoken. Meyer slithered out of his father's way, ceding his position in the family to his brother Jake. Joseph kept to himself, avoiding trouble. The girls were well mannered. Rae, the youngest, was already in school, and she adored Behr. Like many a youngest child, she never received the harsh discipline that the older children experienced.

Best of all, when it was not a school day, Behr now came to the kitchen and waited good-humoredly for Jake to finish his breakfast.

"Ready for a day at the bakery?" the father said, and the son wiped his face and nodded. "Right, Papa!"

Jake needed no urging. He was happier at the bakery than in the high school.

He shared his father's curiosity about machinery—and his father's boundless energy.

Behr had chosen his successor—if he could only keep his anger in check.

* * *

In the year 1901 Behr started the matzo-baking season on the first of January. "The early start of the baking is a blessing," he said to Nesha that morning. "God willing, it's also a good omen for the new century that has just begun."

Everything was new and fresh. The crisp newness of the stationery that Behr brought home and laid out on the big table, where his wife and sons would be sure to see it. Embossed on the top were the words "Office of Behr Manischewitz, Clarke Street."

Behr and Nesha Manischewitz (around 1900).

Behr's charity work was another new thing. He had gone on a long business trip to the East in the fall. As soon as he returned, he turned his attention to charity work. He made full use of the short two months that were left before the cleaning of the ovens began in December.

"The Zionist movement needs our support," he told Nesha in January, "so that it should not fall only under the care of the non-Orthodox."

"The Zionist movement?" Nesha wasn't used to this new interest of Behr's, which sounded so secular.

He nodded, but something else was on his mind.

"You could begin to participate in the women's charities, my good wife," he said.

It wasn't a reprimand. She couldn't have done it sooner with small children in the house. But now it was time.

"I will, God willing," she agreed.

And so in the new century, Nesha made her entry into the women's charitable organizations.

Meanwhile Behr—who had become active too, in several associations, particularly in summer and fall, when the bakery was not functioning—focused much of his attention on improving the process of matzo baking. There were now three different machines involved before the matzo entered the oven, doing the work of a human baker, kneading the dough and cutting and rolling it. And he introduced an electric fan to keep the bakery premises cool. This was no simple matter. Before installing the fan, he had to get rabbinic confirmation that it did not affect the speed of fermentation or otherwise interfere with the process of matzo baking.

Nesha had barely removed her coat at a charity meeting in the spring of 1905, when a woman she knew slightly accosted her.

"Your son Jake, a fine boy, may the evil eye never know it. He must be nearly nineteen now, right?"

"Yes, nineteen." Nesha waited for the story.

"Well. I happen to know he has been seen more than once at the soda parlor at Peeble's Corner, drinking ice cream sodas with his best friend—what's the boy's name, Max?"

"Yes, his friend Max," said Nesha. Peeble's Corner was the social hub of Walnut Hills, the hilltop neighborhood where many of the well-off Jews now lived.

"Together with two very attractive young girls."

"Who are the girls?" came Nesha's eager reply. She wasn't ashamed to ask.

"They're sisters, and they come from a very well-to-do family out on Mount Lookout."

And how did she know about it? The woman shrugged. "In Cincinnati, if you want to know what's going on, you just open your window."

The woman had nothing more to say, so Nesha went to take her seat.

The lecture was about the needy Jews in Palestine, but her thoughts were on the gossip she had just heard. A cold, clammy fear seized her. There were hardly any Jews on Mount Lookout. Was her son seeing a non-Jewish girl? His friend Max was an irreverent young fellow. But her own son? Was it possible? She left the lecture without a word to anyone.

She was very quiet that evening at the dinner table.

"How was your charity meeting?" Behr asked. She looked at him guiltily. "It was all right. The lecture was interesting."

Fortunately he did not ask for details. He smoothed out his napkin pensively on the table. His next words were addressed to his sons:

"After we move over to West Sixth, we'll finally have the whole baking operation in one place." As he spoke, he sketched a design with his fork onto the napkin. Nesha recognized his "invention" behavior.

"You've designed some new equipment for the new bakery," she said.

Behr looked up, surprised. "Right. But only for next season. We move in the summer." He looked into space, as if arranging machinery in the new bakery.

Nesha said nothing about the gossip. But she escaped to her bedroom early and stood at the window while cold fear grasped her. *What if her favorite son married a non-Jewish girl? God forbid such a horror. She had vowed long ago never to treat her future daughter-in-law harshly. But a Gentile woman? If her son married a Gentile woman, Behr would mourn him as dead. Surely God could not intend for such a thing to happen. Was she so undeserving that such a punishment would be meted out to her?*

Jake on his eighteenth birthday, July 6, 1903.

Pearls of sweat had formed on her forehead. She opened her dresser and feverishly reached for her copy of the Book of Psalms. She would read Psalms in every quiet moment, starting right now, until God gave her an answer.

She had to live with her anxiety for nearly a week. The woman who had given her the gossip was sure to find out more details; it was too good an item to leave alone. All week, Nesha planned her itinerary so as to be sure to meet the woman again, "accidentally."

On Thursday, she spent the whole afternoon in Walnut Hills, visiting several shops frequented by women of the neighborhood. Her last stop was at the kosher butcher, crowded with Jewish women buying the meat they would prepare tomorrow for the family's Sabbath meals. As she hoped, the woman with the news about her son was among them. Seeing Nesha, the woman promptly set down her package of meat on the counter and waited for a chance to gossip.

When the butcher went to the rear of the shop, she leaned over to Nesha confidentially. "The two sisters are from the Quitman family, which owns the carriage business on Fifth Street. German Jews. Reformed Jews. And well-off."

Without waiting for Nesha's reaction, she launched into a discussion of how young people today were all hanging out in the soda parlors and speaking slang, "even the Orthodox girls, can you believe it?"

"Yes, and the girls are so outspoken," Nesha said, but she was not really concentrating. She had learned what she needed to know. "Well, I must rush. Have a good Sabbath."

She hastened out of the shop and into the sunlight, which looked a whole lot brighter now.

Her son was drinking sodas with Jewish girls.

* * *

Henrietta's grandchildren all had American names. The Protestant ones, of course. But also Lee's children—his sons, for instance: Harry, Jesse, Arthur, and Walter. And their sisters, all such beautiful young American girls.

The two older ones, Pearl and Stella, were vivacious girls in their teens. They both wore fashionable dresses, and had abundant brown hair, which they curled with a curling iron and combed in the latest fashion. They laughed a lot, and they were usually together. But their faces weren't at all the same. Stella's face was round and mischievous. It seemed to hide nothing.

Pearl's face was oval, and more refined. A hundred different expressions played across it, often in quick succession. Her face showed sensitivity as well as humor. Like her lovely name, Pearl had hidden

depths and a glowing look that was both soft and subtle. She had a
creamy, smooth complexion, and a warm, flashing smile.

Pearl was everyone's dream of a perfect American granddaughter.
Her high school life sounded like a fairy story. Young men awaited her
whenever she stepped out of the school building, inviting her to a
soda fountain, begging for permission to carry her books and escort
her home.

But Henrietta seldom saw her grandchildren nowadays. She still
lived downtown. And she was usually so tired that she could hardly
think of having tea with her friends, let alone make a trip up to
Mount Lookout.

* * *

Sometimes Jake worked different hours from his father and came
home in the daytime. He would head directly for the kitchen.

Nesha had long since acquired a maid to help her with the
housework. But in order to keep a strictly kosher kitchen, she still
preferred to do most of the cooking herself. Whenever her son appeared, she made him a snack, and he stayed to talk.

At first the conversations were about his work at the matzo
bakery. Sometimes she understood the things he told her, and
other times she just enjoyed her son's presence and the way his
work seemed to fascinate him.

Gradually he began to confide in her. She no longer needed to
get reports on his whereabouts from her women friends.

She learned that they were a foursome—her son Jake, his
buddy Max, and the two girls, whose names were Pearl and Stella.
She wasn't too pleased about his long-term friendship with Max.
The young man was a distant cousin and so could not be avoided,
but he had a sly, provocative sort of smile. Behr had given him
work in the matzo factory. But work was one thing, and character was another.

The following year, and for two more years after that, the foursome were still together.

"You aren't jealous, Mama, that I buy my girl candies?" Jake looked at his mother anxiously. "My dear boy, of course not," she said. Jake still offered his mother candies from time to time.

He described his latest outing with Pearl. They'd taken an evening steamboat ride to the amusement park at Coney Island. The new amusement park was reputed to be just as exciting as the one in New York that it was named for, which itself was still a novelty.

It was a fantasy world for Nesha. All afternoon in the kitchen her mind was pleasantly filled with images of her son's courtship of this lucky girl. How he would take her arm as he led her down the torch-lit ramp at the public landing by the riverfront. How she would laugh as she let him help her, and how she would call him "Jack," as all of her son's friends did. How they would board the steamboat, the *Island Queen*, which would be brightly lit up with gas lamps, and it would take them with all the other young merrymakers upstream to the amusement park.

One noontime Jake leaned against the kitchen counter, too keyed up to sit down, while his mother tranquilly peeled potatoes.

"Mama, sometimes I don't know which one I prefer, Pearl or her sister Stella," he said.

"Pearl has more style, but Stella is, well, um."

He paused. Stella was really something in her red bathing costume. Sometimes he couldn't keep his hands off her, sneaking a kiss, fondling her wet breasts under the water. Jake didn't tell his mother about the bathing beach, so as not shock her.

In fact, she was not quite as ignorant as he thought. She knew about the bathing beach. And she saw the fire in his eyes when he spoke about Stella.

* * *

Nesha said nothing about these developments to her husband, whose attention was focused on the bakery.

He was receiving orders from all over the country now, and even from Europe. He traveled a lot to get new customers.

"You're your own best salesman," Nesha said.

He nodded, looking very pleased and proud. "I have to be," he said. "A matzo company is a pious undertaking. Selling matzos is different from selling soap."

"Don't I know it," Nesha agreed. Proctor and Gamble had started when young Mr. Gamble set up a tiny shop on Sixth Street and walked over with a bucket to the nearby slaughterhouse, where he got permission to muck around up to his knees in pig's gore to get the fat he needed for soap making. The Milling Machine Company, known today as Milacron, had started from a little nuts-and-bolts workshop on the third floor of a downtown building. Then one day the machine that made the screws broke down. The owner made his own machine out of necessity, and moved on to large-scale machine manufacturing.

But to sell matzos, you had to make people understand that matzos were a product, that their rabbi did not need to make his own matzos anymore. So the Jewish institutions themselves had to change. Luckily for Behr, this change was taking place. The rabbis no longer controlled all facets of Jewish life as they had in Europe. *Mikvah* and burial, aid for the poor, and many other communal functions were no longer the rabbis' sole responsibility.

The change did not happen overnight. Behr had to assure the grocers and rabbis that they could rely on his piety to guarantee them a truly kosher product. He had begun traveling years earlier. He went farther from home now, but the principle was still the same. He was marketing himself, Behr Manischewitz, together with the matzos.

The matzo bakery on Sixth Street, Cincinnati.

Jake found his mother in the kitchen on the morning after Behr's departure for Detroit. She was shaping biscuits with floury hands and humming over her work.

"Mama, you look so sad that Father's away," he teased. "No shirts to iron twice a day just the way he wants them—is that what you're missing?" Nesha blushed. "Your father has to travel," she protested.

"And we have to do our jobs while he's gone." Jake patted his mother's hand, then dusted the flour off his own hand with a flourish. "I'm off to the bakery now."

Nesha remained where she was standing and listened to the thud of the front door and the reverberation of her son's rapid footsteps as he headed down the steps and out to the street until she could hear him no longer.

Was it a sin to love her son so dearly?

Last night she had dreamed of her son. She was standing behind him, combing his black curls over and over as she used to do when he was a boy. Only in the dream he was not a boy, but grown, and the beautiful pearl-handled comb in her hand had not existed in his boyhood. She had awakened uneasy, as though caught in a forbidden act. Now the morning sun streamed in as if to reassure her of her innocence. How could loving her own son be sinful? She would make a cherry pie today, the younger children's favorite. She set about it immediately. Nobody would be shortchanged due to her love for Jake.

In case she needed a sign from heaven of her blamelessness, she received it upon Behr's return. While in Detroit, he'd heard about the healing qualities of the water of the spa in Mount Clemens, Michigan, where there were many Jewish clients.

"You will go to Mount Clemens this summer for the cure, God willing," he told Nesha. "And every summer thereafter. You won't be so tired after you take the waters."

"You think it will be healthy? Then I'll go, God willing!" Nesha already had a big smile on her face. She was thinking of the resort at Polangen, now known as Palanga, that much-coveted, almost mythical resort up the coast from Memel. Her girlhood dream, at last to be fulfilled.

"It's scientifically proven," Behr said. "And the hotel has kosher food." Nesha blushed. She had forgotten to ask about the food.

She luxuriated at the spa for three weeks that summer. And indeed, she felt less tired, as she would after each visit to the spa. Whether this was due to its medicinal benefits—or the pleasant release from the daily stress at home—did not really matter. Behr seemed as pleased to have her there as if he had invented the scientifically proven waters himself.

"I want to know if the waters are doing you good," he wrote, at the end of the first week. "Please send a photograph to me so that I can see that you look well, may you live long years, my dear wife."

And so she had her photograph taken by the hotel's photographer, feeling both embarrassed and coy, for she had never been photographed without her husband at her side. The photograph showed a relaxed-looking, plump middle-aged woman with a wide smile. Behr would be satisfied.

In March 1907, Behr enlarged the bakery again. He purchased the adjoining Bing bakery, which was larger and had a lot of equipment already installed. Some of it had to be adapted to the special art of matzo baking. Behr made his own designs for the ovens and the other machinery.

The buildings were five stories tall, and joined together they included over 37,000 square feet of floor space, exclusively for matzos. There was a double set of machinery so that one set could be cleaned while the other was in use. With both sets in use, Behr could produce over 20,000 pounds of matzos in a single day.

And the procedure was patented—how proud he was when he received his first patent! It was through his visits to the Milling Machine Company that he had learned, almost accidentally, about the U.S. Patent Office and the way one must apply. Not many immigrants knew how to do this. His non-Jewish friend at the Milling Machine had walked him through the entire proce-

Nesha at the spa in Mt. Clemens.

dure. He showed his patent to his son Jake and explained the process to him.

"There will be a need for more of these patents," he explained. "It's something you'll need to know later on."

I'll need to know how to make patents? Jake was too surprised at his father's evidently high opinion of him to even think of replying.

When the bakery moved into the new premises, Behr placed a big advertisement in the *American Israelite*. Every Jew in Cincinnati saw the ad. It was a landmark event.

The year 1907 was also the year in which Nesha and Behr turned fifty. They never celebrated birthdays, not even for the children. This was an American custom that, though not exactly forbidden, didn't seem to fit in with tradition and was therefore (at least in Behr's view) best ignored.

Even so, turning fifty gave Nesha something to think about. Was she doing all she should for others, now that her family was mostly grown? If she were selfish and self-satisfied, she might attract God's punishment. Better not take such a risk. And so she increased her charity work, which after all was not an unpleasant chore. She enjoyed attending the Ladies Benevolent Society, where she was looked upon as one of the more prominent ladies, at least by the East European women.

Activities or not, she usually managed to be at home in the kitchen when Jake breezed in for his mid-day break, and listened to whatever he wanted to tell her.

"Father's new gas-fired ovens allow you to control the heat precisely, and the baking speed, too. It means you can control the consistency of the matzos and the quality is always up to standard."

He watched as she leaned over her old-fashioned oven to take out a sheet of muffins.

"I thought it was because the matzos are square now?" said Nesha. She set down the muffins, and a delicious cinnamon aroma filled the kitchen.

"The square matzos were one of Father's smartest inventions." Jake reached for one of his mother's non-standard muffins and bit into it with relish.

"They're square first of all so as to make it easier to pack them in boxes. But it's also so that you don't need to waste the part that has to be trimmed off. In your ordinary pastry, you just take the part that you trim off and reuse it."

"Or else I let my little boy eat it, a little bit won't hurt him," Nesha said. She looked fondly upwards at her little boy.

"But with matzos, Mama, you know that you can't do that. Because you might keep the dough for too long, and it would begin to rise, and that isn't allowed."

Square matzos–an early box design.

"Even when you know the reason," said Nesha, "it takes a while to get used to a square matzo." She looked at her muffins. "A woman needs time to get used to change."

A woman liked to arrange the Passover table exactly the way her mother had done. Luckily it was the men who decided this particular question. The men knew that Behr's matzos were strictly kosher, and the shape did not matter.

"Anyway," said Jake, and paused to finish off the muffin, "anyway, Father has enough new ideas to keep us on our toes. He's going this afternoon to the Milling Machine Company again. So I'd better get myself back over to the bakery now. I'll have to take over for him."

Jake wiped the crumbs from his hands and rushed out.

Nesha put the muffins aside, and opened the pantry to decide on the evening's menu.

If Behr was at the Milling Machine, he'd be late for dinner.

He would linger there as long as possible, observing the machines that had been ordered for other customers, and chatting with the owner or the men, in order to get new ideas.

Behr's ideas were not just mechanical. He also had ideas for increasing the range of products. The first products to be added were matzo meal and farfel.

He had got both of these ideas from watching Nesha. He'd seen how she wrapped matzos in a cloth and smashed them to make soup nuts, called farfel, and how she ground them to make the equivalent of breadcrumbs, to replace the forbidden flour.

"We could sell those already made," he told her one day in the kitchen. And by the next Passover season, he was marketing both new products.

* * *

By this time the older children had reached—and passed—the age that Nesha and Behr considered appropriate for marriage. Yet they were all still unmarried.

Mayme had refused more than one proposal, so what more could be done for her? She was too outspoken—that seemed to be the problem. She had opinions on everything—Zionism, women's suffrage, bicycles—and she shared her ideas with everyone, including Behr's dinner guests, to his great displeasure.

Their sons' bachclorhood was a worse affront to Behr, for he cared desperately about ensuring the future of the family and the matzo business. But there was no way he could impose his will on the three older boys.

Jake was twenty-three. He worked hard alongside his father in the bakery, but his sentimental life was his own. Any suggestion of parental matchmaking was sure to bring on a furious refusal— Behr had already attempted it once or twice, with that result.

The case of Jake's brother Meyer was worse, for he was two years older than Jake, and showed no signs of even looking for a wife. But Behr had already given up on Meyer. As long as Meyer put in a full day's work at the factory and showed up at the synagogue, Behr left him alone.

He also usually left his third son alone. "Joseph isn't mature enough to marry," he said, and did not explain further.

The future of their sons Max and Hirsh in the Holy Land was much more easily settled. Max reached the marriageable age of seventeen in February 1907. By springtime a good match was found for him, a girl from a pious family.

The arrangements were completed in May. In June, Behr told Nesha his plans.

"The wedding will be in July, God willing. It is the only time of year that I can leave the bakery. We shall attend the wedding in Jerusalem."

"In Jerusalem?" she echoed. It sounded unreal.

And yet one warm afternoon, Nesha sat down in the bay window to pack. She remained seated for a while with the open trunk before her, looking at the piles of clothing.

A wave of memory washed over her, filling the sunlit room, with its overstuffed sofa and ample closets of highly polished walnut. *I haven't sat all alone in a quiet room since I was a girl in Memel.*

Twenty-two years had gone by since she had packed all their possessions on the last night in Memel. They hadn't even had a trunk, only a motley array of bags and battered suitcases. She mentally compared the young woman she was then with the plump, middle-aged one she was now, who could choose from a whole closet full of dresses the ones to pack for an ocean voyage.

She had not traveled much in all these years. Only to the spa and some nearby towns. Behr had traveled a lot around the country, promoting his matzos to grocers in many cities where Jews lived. But this would be his first and only trip to the Holy Land.

After a pleasant half hour alone with her thoughts, she finished packing, feeling pleased with herself. Soon she would be a rich lady boarding a ship, and it was for a good purpose—a mitzvah, Behr said: marrying a son was a mitzvah.

The voyage amazed them both. Their arrival at the small, sleepy-looking port of Jaffa, where many Arabs were walking around in their long robes, had a dreamlike quality. Then they traveled through the exotic countryside, the Sharon Valley with its citrus fruits and exotic plants. They reached the dry, sun-bleached hills, and then at last Jerusalem itself, rising up on its hillside.

Everything about the city of Jerusalem was remarkable. Nesha was bestowed with impressions so rich that she would be unable to sort them all out in her mind for years to come. The clean, whitewashed look of the stone buildings, the narrow alleys that on closer view revealed glimpses of poverty as miserable as any poverty in Lithuania. The blue skies and the blinding sunlight, with little white clouds drifting by, close enough to touch, but never releasing the tiniest drop of rain. The Wailing Wall, rising up high above the narrow alley that one had to walk in order to approach it.

And then at last Max and Hirsh, her sons, stood before her. They wore the long, loose clothing of pious young men in the Holy Land. Nesha greeted them shyly, hardly believing that they were her own sons.

Seventeen-year-old Max had made an easy transition when he exchanged his American schoolboy clothes for the quaint ones of the yeshiva student. He had donned his Hebrew name as easily as the new clothes, and he had made himself a place among the local boys—not through scholarship, but in whatever ways boys did this when left to their own devices. Max knew how to look out for himself.

Nesha questioned him about his bride-to-be, Edith, when Behr was out of their hearing, feeling very modern as she did so.

"Are you satisfied with this Edith?" she asked. "Have you met her, do you like her?"

"She's fine, Mama, don't worry."

The family was ushered into a room where Edith sat demurely with her parents.

Max winked at the girl when he thought nobody was looking. Edith tossed her hair back proudly, ignoring him with a verve that made Nesha smile. There was a pact between her son and this closely watched Jerusalem girl. They were accomplices, biding their time till the adults around them left and their life could begin.

Hirsh, almost sixteen, made the biggest impression on his mother. His earnestness when he talked about his studies had to be real. Nesha had already thought this must be so when she read his letters. But letters were nothing compared to the boy she now saw before her.

Her thoughts went back to the day his father had chosen him for the journey. She had been so relieved at her Jake's escape from

Hirsh at sixteen.

his fate that she had packed up little Hirsh's things without a word of protest.

What if she had cried, pleaded, made a scene, told Behr the boy was ill or feverish, or some other pretext? A woman could influence a husband when she really wanted to. But she hadn't done it—not for Hirsh. Over the years the face of the wide-eyed eight-year-old had reproached her.

Now the uneasiness she had borne, and the guilt she had felt for perhaps—God forbid—devoting less love than she might have to her younger sons, was shed in an instant. She enjoyed the wedding thoroughly. The customs were a little different from the ones she knew, but many things were the same. The marriage canopy was held above their heads by four pious young men in shiny black coats. As the groom's mother, Nesha stood in her place of honor. And when the ceremony closed in song and dance, she felt an unexpected thrill at the familiar words of the song: "The hills of Judah will resound with joy, and the voices of bride and bridegroom will be heard." For the hills of Judah were real, and she had seen them.

She left Jerusalem after the wedding with a sense of having lived through an experience she had never expected to be part of her life's journey.

On the return voyage, she leaned back contentedly on her deck chair, watching the sea for many pleasant hours. She imagined the vast globe, crisscrossed with long traces made by the two journeys of her lifetime, from Memel to Cincinnati, and now to Jerusalem and back.

Behr used the time on the ship for study ("Such an opportunity to study! At home a man is not so free!")

He wouldn't sit with her and watch the ocean. It was written in the Talmud that a man should not even look up from his studies to say "What a beautiful tree!" A pious man's thoughts were on a higher plane than a woman's. And so his wife was left to chat on the deck with the other women passengers. Sometimes, though, she looked up from her chair and saw her husband standing nearby, breathing in deeply as though the fresh salt air pleased him very much.

Hirsh was given a bride the next year, in December of 1908. Behr had made the preliminary contacts for this marriage while they were in Jerusalem, though the girl was from Petach-Tikva. Nesha and Behr would not be able to travel to the Holy Land for a second wedding. Behr bought the newlyweds some land near Petach-Tikva with orange groves. He told Nesha that it was important to buy land in the Holy Land, so that it could eventually become a Jewish state.

Nesha was skeptical. "How can there be a Jewish state? With Jewish policemen, and an army?"

"There are Jewish farmers already," he said. "And in fact, some of the policemen that you saw in Jerusalem, wearing the Turkish uniform, were Jews. So perhaps one day, with God's help, there will be a Jewish state too."

The purchase of land for Hirsh and his young wife was Behr's statement of hope. And it seemed for a while that this branch of the family would take root in the Holy Land, like their newly planted orange groves.

But the young couple were not destined to live on their land. The unfortunate young bride died of childbed fever in November of the very next year, ten days after giving birth to a son. And Hirsh returned hastily to Jerusalem with the baby, to stay with his brother's in-laws.

"My grief is very great," he wrote to his parents soon afterward. "But it was God's will to take my Leah so quickly, and I must accept it. Now I am in Jerusalem so that my brother Max's family can care for my poor motherless son. They will arrange a new marriage for me next year, God willing, and with Father's agreement, for it is wrong to remain alone and grieve, when my son needs a mother's care." In August 1910, Hirsh's second wedding was held in Jerusalem. Hirsh was nineteen, his new bride Sarah was sixteen.

* * *

In 1908, Jake was still not sure which of the two sisters he would marry.

On Sundays, or whenever he was not working, he would go over to the big white house on Mount Lookout together with his buddy Max, both of them smartly dressed, not looking like immigrant boys (or at least, he hoped not). And yet, there was something about him that gave away his origin. Maybe it was the way he spoke so passionately, no matter what the subject, or the way he gestured with his hands, whether to make a point or simply to smooth back his unruly black hair.

Usually they stood around the yard and chatted for a while with any of the brothers who happened to be there, pretending that this was the purpose of the visit. Pearl and her sister Stella never came downstairs immediately.

At last Pearl and Stella would make their appearance in the yard, freshly dressed in long cotton dresses and beribboned summer hats. Then there was a lively discussion of the choice of destination for the afternoon's outing, after which they all left merrily, waving gaily to the girls' mama or anyone else in the yard.

* * *

Jake was ashamed later of the way he treated the two sisters. He flirted with both of them. And once, he did more than that.

He found himself alone with Stella one summer day—Pearl had excused herself—in a bower down below the house, hidden from view. "Let's be naughty," Stella said, in her naughtiest possible voice. She was wearing a shiny, smooth dress, and how could a man resist? Stella leaned against a tree and let him caress her, within shouting distance of the house. It was possibly the most dangerous thing he had done in his entire life.

Moments later they climbed up the slope and walked around to the front of the house. The girls' grandmother was watching from a chair on the front lawn. Did she guess what he'd been up to? She looked far too old to think about such things. He waved innocently. Stella, irrepressible, winked at him.

Would Stella tell Pearl what they had done? The next Saturday afternoon at the park, he placed his arm a little too boldly around Pearl's waist. "Don't you misbehave with *me*, you bad boy," she said, and he quickly removed the arm.

He was left to guess whether Pearl knew about his misbehavior. He silently swore he would never tell anyone, not even Max, who, as it turned out, had also had his way with Stella. Unlike Jake, Max saw no reason to refrain from boasting about it.

* * *

Nesha would never in her lifetime decide which way of making a marriage was the better one: an arranged marriage or a marriage of love. The freedom to choose his own bride wasn't making a happy young man of her favorite son. He'd decided, finally, which one of the two sisters he wanted to marry. It was Pearl— but she hadn't accepted. She had some foolish idea about acting on the stage.

Jake told his mother about the theater troupe where Pearl performed. He described her latest costume in detail. "Spangles, lace, and frills, Mother, you would love it."

Then he turned serious.

"Pearl is thinking of dedicating her whole life to acting."

Nesha couldn't believe it. "Your Pearl is a modern girl, she wants to amuse herself for a while in this daring way, but when all is said and done, a young girl wants to marry."

Jake shook his head despairingly.

In January of 1909, Nesha sent up a silent prayer for her son. *This year, dear God, let my son wed his destined bride.*

As the winter progressed, things seemed to be going his way.

Jake had made a hit with Pearl's entire family. There would be no problem in convincing her parents to accept Jake as a son-in-law. "You know, Mama," Jake said, "Pearl's old man, Lee, owns a big carriage business downtown."

Nesha did not say that she had learned this long ago from her spies.

"He gives the girls cheap costume jewelry that nobody would ever want to wear. Can you imagine that, Mama? What a miser!" Jake's own father had given his daughters only a few pieces of jewelry, but each piece was real gold.

By this time, Jake was visiting the house on Mount Lookout almost daily.

He often brought a box of the best chocolates and distributed them to the whole family. Pearl's little sisters adored him, and he soon developed a comradely relationship with her brothers.

When Pearl was performing in a play, excitement filled the big white house on Mount Lookout. One or more of her brothers would usually accompany her to wherever the theater company was rehearsing. The brothers would report on the play's progress from week to week, and they would describe all of the performers, and the stage play, endlessly, to the rest of the family.

After a dress rehearsal Pearl sometimes came home with her theatrical makeup still on, so that they could all admire her, which they did. Only their grandmother Henrietta, who still lived downtown, was usually absent from these gatherings.

Around Christmastime in 1908, Pearl played the role of a fairy princess, and looked indeed fairy-like in her shiny white dress, with the gossamer wings attached to the back of her costume. She held a silvery scepter with a crinkled golden half-moon upon it.

On the day of the dress rehearsal, her brothers took her to a professional photographer.

The photograph was placed on display in the front hall, for all to admire.

* * *

In the spring of 1909, when she was twenty, Pearl appeared in another play. Pearl laughed when her mother asked to see the photograph. It was the rich, deep laughter of an actress whose voice was a fine-tuned instrument.

"I don't think you will want a photograph this time, Ma. I will be playing the role of La Trochard, the old hag."

Maybe she was only an old hag, but after a performance or two, she was more set than ever on an acting career. She said she aimed to go to New York to act in the "real" theater. After this an-

RABBI DOV BER MANISCHEWITZ

Samples of the Passover menu plans and recipes for everyday kosher meals provided over the years by the B. Manischewitz

"EVERY YEAR FOR NEARLY HALF A CENTURY BILKER'S HAS FEATURED MANISCHEWITZ!"

says NAT REIS, guiding head of BILKER'S in Cincinnati. "When George Bilker opened his first store in 1906, he featured Manischewitz, and so has every Bilker store since then."

Top:
A fanciful version of the House of Manischewitz. Matzo construction contests have been held up into the twenty-first century.

Left:
Nat Reis, a Cincinnati grocer, shows off his display of Manischewitz products for the September 1955 issue of Food Store Review

nouncement, there were endless discussions around the dinner table, and they all went exactly the same way.

As soon as Pearl said the words "New York," her father would say, "No way are you going to New York."

One of Pearl's brothers would break right in on cue: "She has the talent for it, why must you try and stop her?"

It was Pearl's mother who usually closed the conversation. "In the end she'll do as her father says, so don't you all waste your breath. Who wants more potatoes?"

The matter seemed to swing first one way, then the other.

* * *

In May Jake suffered a discouraging setback. He came into the kitchen waving a small clipping from the newspaper.

"Mama, Pearl is going to leave for New York to become an actress! I will never accept it, damn it, never, I tell you! See for yourself!"

Nesha took the clipping, which included a photo of Pearl in an elaborate costume, and began to read the few lines below the photo. She couldn't read fast enough. He snatched it back and read in tragic tones:

Got her Way: Talented young actress Pearl Quitman has overcome parental objections and embarked upon a professional stage career. She will leave in June for New York and join one of Henry Savage's companies.

He paused poignantly, waiting for his mother's reaction.

For a moment she was silent, drawn in by her son's despair. Then she recovered. "How can she go to New York alone? She won't do it. She got in a play, on the stage, the people all applauded, so it goes to her head. By June, she'll forget it. A fine young man, a handsome one like my son with a romantic heart and a good head, proposes to her. She will forget it."

Nesha looked at her son adoringly, but of course, this was no help.

The next morning he took a taxi up to Mount Lookout.

"Hello Jack, where's the fire?" shouted one of the younger sisters from somewhere in the yard.

"Pearl isn't here," chimed in the smallest sister. Pearl's silhouette was distinctly visible in a second-story window.

Jack shifted nervously from one foot to the other, waiting for Pearl to come out.

After a while Pearl came downstairs and invited Jack to sit in the parlor with her. They stayed in the house for an hour or two. Then he came out, looking just as troubled as when he came in, and left without a word to any of the family members who were still in the yard.

* * *

Pearl's troupe agreed to put on a performance a week or two later for the convicts at the workhouse. She told her family about it over dinner. They were suitably taken aback.

"Poor things, they seldom get any real amusement, do they?" Pearl said. She enjoyed shocking her family, and she would not have another chance to do it, not in this life. The performance for the convicts was to be Pearl's last stage performance ever.

But Jake didn't know this. He moped all through the spring, allowing his mother to serve him his favorite foods, which he ate mechanically.

Sometimes he ranted about Pearl's brothers: "Mama, they are actually *encouraging* her to go to New York. By God, I expected some loyalty from them!"

* * *

Pearl sat at her desk, looking out over the yard and the broad oak trees that beckoned down toward the Ohio River far below, glinting under a hot sun. It was a quiet morning at the house on Mount Lookout. Her mother was busy in the yard with her everlasting chickens. Her boyfriend Jack was at work downtown, sweltering over his ovens.

She wrote a few lines, then leaned back and looked at what she'd written. The letter was addressed to her sister-in-law Rae, her favorite confidante.

I think I shall give up the stage entirely.
Father and all my friends object so strongly to it, that I am discouraged. And I really have discovered I have no talent for the profession, even if I am flattered once in a while . . .

She paused and nibbled the pen, her mouth forming a pretty little pout. Was it only flattery? And if so, did it mean she wasn't a real actress? She was taking the easy path now. She would marry Jake, and after all, she loved him. He would shower her with his love, and she would have fine things, a good life. And wasn't that what really mattered most? Still—she hesitated at the final act, to tell Jack her decision and close the door forever on acting. Or maybe she just enjoyed seeing Jack's anxiety, which flattered her more than a whole theater full of spectators.

* * *

A few days later, Jake reported the half-good news to his mother. "Mama, Pearl has decided to give up the stage. She announced it to her whole family."

"So that she can marry you, right?" Nesha was ready to celebrate. But Jake raised a warning hand.

"I think so, Mama, but damn! I can't be sure!" He thumped his hand on the table. "She hasn't said a word to me."

"Maybe you should talk to her now. A girl doesn't need *too* much time."

Nesha's anxiety matched her son's. She knew the drama would be played out in just a few weeks.

But June came to an end with no news about Pearl.

Chapter 5

Let Her Rejoice

Let the barren city be jubilantly happy and joyful at her joyous reunion with her children. You are blessed, Lord, who makes Zion rejoice with her children.
Let the loving couple be very happy, just as You made Your creation happy in the garden of Eden, so long ago. You are blessed, Lord, who makes the bridegroom and the bride happy.

—*from the Jewish marriage ceremony*

July. The sun beat down upon the house, and Jake's tension hung in air. His birthday was on the sixth, but it gave him no cheer.

Nesha took her time about preparing for her annual cure at the baths in Mount Clemens. Going to the spa was a privilege she loved. The cure lasted for three delicious weeks, and this time would be special: Jake had promised to join her for the third week. But with no word on his engagement, she left for Mount Clemens without her usual enthusiasm. When her son arrived, would he be joyful or brokenhearted?

After a moody day on the train, her spirits rose when she entered the familiar lobby of the Hotel Medea. She unpacked hastily and made her way down the carpeted hallway to the white Italian tiled foyer of the luxurious bathhouse. When at last the sulfurous water plumped up her sagging breasts and lightened her heavy body, she felt blissfully relieved.

In the evening she dressed for dinner and joined a group of friends. They were mostly Jewish women her own age, from Cincinnati and Pittsburgh and Chicago, who came each year, as she did, for the cure.

She wore a huge hat, which she had bought when she discovered that Jake found Pearl's oversized hats enormously attractive. Her friends at the spa admired her clothes and hat and shared all the latest gossip with her. But she could not shake off her worries about her son. When he failed to write immediately, her anxiety increased. By the end of the second week, she was feeling very downhearted. She occasionally allowed herself a good cry, which made her eyes red, and that was how Jake found her when he arrived on the nineteenth of July.

Jake came in like a whirlwind with an exuberant group of young men from Detroit whom he had met on the train.

As soon as he saw his mother in the lobby, he left them without a word of explanation and flew to where she was sitting. He took both her hands in his own with a flourish, and gave her his biggest smile.

"My dear little Mama, what's the matter? Are you lonesome for your long-lost loving son?"

Nesha lost her woebegone look in an instant. There was no need to ask how things had gone with Pearl. She knew from her son's voice that everything was all right.

"Dinner is at six," she told him. "Enough time for us both to freshen up." Neither of them mentioned her red eyes.

At dinner that first evening they talked about anything and everything. Being so far from home made conversation freer.

They talked about the spa and how its waters were being boiled down and bottled as medicine. The water was a popular conversational topic with the guests at the spa.

"I may bring home a bottle of it to drink. Though it tastes awful," Nesha said with a grimace. "Did your father tell you he got a letter from your brother Max in Jerusalem? He's coming to

Cincinnati next month with his wife, to stay here. He wants to work in the bakery."

Jake shrugged. "Well, why not? There's enough work for him— we can rely on Father for that."

The brother who had been ten years old when he left, and was now nineteen, was not a part of Jake's world.

When dinner was over, they went together to one of the springs, which was ornamented by a garden with wrought-iron tables and chairs, where it was customary to drink a quart or more of spring water. The other diners also got up and headed for the garden.

This ritual took some two hours, during which a small orchestra played, to help the water go down more easily. Jake and his mother talked some more.

At last they talked about Pearl.

"Mama, I thought you knew how things stood with your long-suffering son," he said. "Otherwise I would have written to spare you the worry. Didn't Father write to you about the ring?"

Nesha shook her head. "What ring?"

"The diamond ring for Pearl. I bought it last week, for three hundred and sixty-two dollars, as soon as I knew she would accept it. The jeweler called Father on the phone, because the ring was so expensive, and he wanted to be sure it was all right. I couldn't stop him."

Behr had given his agreement in order to avoid scandal. But he had written nothing to Nesha about his son's purchase.

"Your father's last letter was very short."

Now she knew the reason for Behr's terseness. He must be furious over Jake's buying the ring without asking his blessing. Not because of the expense. Behr believed in buying quality. But he would need to be mollified.

She sipped another glass of spring water, while Jake got up to dance. Even as a newly engaged young man, he couldn't easily refuse to dance, when all the young girls at the spa—mostly Jewish girls from Cincinnati or Detroit chaperoned by their mothers—expected it.

Sitting there in comfort, with her son happily dancing and music playing, she felt a twinge of guilt as she realized that Behr was not just angry: he was in dark despair over what he didn't know and was too proud to ask: was his son's fiancée Jewish? Suddenly she was unsympathetic. If Behr hadn't been so stern and forbidding, he would have known about Pearl for years. His anguish was his own fault.

On the second night, they discussed Jake's immediate future. First he must introduce Pearl to his parents, and then fix the date for the wedding. There was one more detail—Pearl had yet to accept the ring. She had pretty much assured him of it. But Jake was excited, volatile, entirely taken up by his passion, so that each of the items on the "to do" list seemed to him like a mountain to be climbed.

He shook his head dramatically.

"To meet you! Yes, by God, I wanted her to come up here to Mount Clemens and meet you first, before Father. Would that have been so difficult? She wouldn't have to stay at the Medea with us; she could stay at one of the other hotels. What was immoral about that, I ask you?"

He gave his mother no time to reply.

"But her father has refused, look here." Jake pulled a letter from his pocket and read it out loud, imitating Lee's gruff voice: "Pearl is okay, Jack, it would not be proper for her to come to you, people would talk."

Nesha looked at the letter, which was scribbled on a page from the note pad of Lee's carriage business. "He doesn't write English any better than I do!" she exclaimed. "And after three generations in America."

She shook her head disapprovingly.

"I never will understand those German Jews. Though I had a friend once, a very kind woman named Henrietta who helped me when we were new in this country. Anyhow, it's no matter if Pearl can't come. I'll meet her at the same time as Father, when we get back to Cincinnati."

"It's the best we can do, then."

Actually, unknown to her son, Nesha had already met Pearl. The two women had met in Eden Park over a year before through what would have appeared to any bystander to be an entirely accidental encounter. "I'm not here to frighten you or give you a hard time," she had said to Pearl with a friendly smile. "What I want is to know the girl my son spends his time with." Pearl had replied graciously, though she could have taken offense. They'd chatted a while, and parted as good friends.

For the rest of the week Jake was floating on air. He wrote letters to Pearl at least every day, sometimes twice a day.

He hung about the lobby waiting for the mail.

One of Pearl's letters so excited him that he sat his mother right down in the lobby and read it to her aloud. It was a sweet letter, and Pearl had not forgotten, at the end, to ask him to send warm greetings to his mother. When he finished, he kissed the page dramatically. "My love, the darlingest girl anywhere!"

One morning he carelessly left an unfinished letter upon the desk in the sitting room. Nesha's eye fell on the page. Had he deliberately left it out, to allow her the secret, vicarious pleasure of reading it? Nesha had never seen a love letter in her life. This one was written in a large, flowery hand.

My Most Precious Jewel,
Just received your Darling letter, and may the good God bless you for it. I greatly wonder if my letters have as much effect on you as yours on me?
Dearest! You are the One and Only One girl for me, and I hope you consider the same of me. And you shall be rewarded for it as long as you live, with the Lovingest, Truest, Most Loyal and Devoted Husband one can find! This is not only my promise but my vow . . .

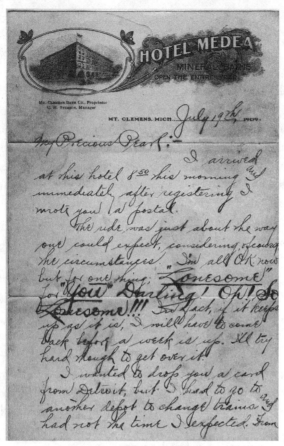

Letter from Jake to Pearl during their courtship.

That was where the page ended. Nesha flushed and turned away quickly, knowing she should not be reading it at all. Her son, in love with a lovely young actress—it was all so beautiful.

* * *

As soon as they returned from the spa, Jake announced the news to his father. As Nesha had advised him, he came right to the point:

"Pearl is Jewish, Papa. Her family are German Jews, and they own the big carriage and livery business down on East Fifth Street, near Sycamore. She went to Walnut Hills High School." He left out the part about Pearl's theatrical career.

Nesha saw the enormous relief in her husband's eyes. He had indeed been suffering over the dire prospect of his son bringing home a Gentile girl. For he had done his own research and made a visit to the carriage business on East Fifth Street. There he had seen the girl's father, a rough-speaking man with leather boots and a cowboy hat. A pagan ornament—actually the Rotary Club emblem—adorned the wall. Knowing little about assimilated German Jews, Behr had left in torment, certain that the man was not Jewish.

Jake brought Pearl to the house the next day. Some other visitors arrived shortly afterwards, so there was no time for any unpleasant interrogation of the young couple.

There was only one moment when Nesha sensed danger, and it came from an unexpected quarter.

One of the guests was Jake's good buddy Max, who was employed by Behr at the matzo factory. A sort of electricity passed between Max and Pearl as he entered the room. Nesha felt it immediately. Pearl saw Nesha watching her and turned red. Then she quickly turned her head to speak to the person next to her. The moment passed. Nobody else had seen it.

After the visitors left, Jake sat down with his father to discuss the details of the wedding. Nesha stayed in the room, prudently hovering in the background.

"Pearl and I will be married on Sunday, August 29th, at three in the afternoon," Jake announced, adding quickly, "at Odd Fellows Temple."

It was a hall used by the Reformed Jews for weddings and other gatherings. Nesha already knew about it. She expected an outburst from Behr, but to her surprise, he said very little.

Even so, Behr was not going to let it go.

"You will stop at our rabbi's home on your way to your temple nonsense. And there you will sign a proper marriage contract. And you will do whatever else the rabbi asks of you." Jake nodded.

"And another thing," Behr continued. "The marriage announcement in the paper will not mention the temple. You will just say, 'The wedding was held privately.' On the personal invitations, you do as you like."

"Yes, Father." Jake looked at his father with respect, to Behr's satisfaction. He would have been less satisfied if he could read his son's thoughts: *How cagey of Father to think of all the angles.*

Nesha's coaching had paid off.

A few days before the wedding, Nesha sent Pearl a letter. She asked one of the younger children to help her with the English. Then she did a final version, which she showed to nobody:

To My dear future Daughter Pearl,
On this occasion of your marriage to my son, I am happy with my husband to wish you happiness and all of the good things in life. You are going to enter the state of marriage which is a Jewish woman's greatest joy, and I hope that you will have many sons and with God's help will live a long life together and be a loving helpmate to your husband, who will cherish you too. Now I am wishing you good luck, and a very warmest heartfelt welcome to our family. With all of my love, from your Mother Nesha
P.S. Only one thing. Be careful my girl a woman must not look at another man. My boy will love you dearly but do not never, ever make him jealous. You know what I mean. I will not say this again. I know I will not need to.

Nesha's hand shook as she sealed the letter. Would her American daughter-in-law be angry? Would she misunderstand?

* * *

When Pearl received Nesha's letter, she went right up to her room and took out the velvet-lined box where she kept her correspondence, to purge it of letters that might seem compromising.

She destroyed several notes from Max, and if she kissed them first, and then felt silly, it didn't matter. Nobody on this earth would ever know about it.

Keeping this small flame alive in her heart, but hidden from all, would soon become second nature to her.

Then she tore up some letters from two of her best buddies from her acting days with the Forepaugh Stock Company, because she thought they might easily be misinterpreted as love letters, although she was quite sure they were not. She kept only the postcards they had sent her when the troupe went away on tour.

And then she looked mournfully out the window, saying goodbye to her lost freedom.

But she was perhaps a better actress than she realized. For even as she felt desolate, a part of her was watching her own performance of heartbreak, nodding and approving as she played out her role. It was not the heartbreak of a simpler young woman.

* * *

After presenting Pearl to his parents, Jake gave her the expensive diamond ring he had bought in June. He gave her the receipt too—for safekeeping, or to show off?—he wasn't sure which. Pearl smoothed it out carefully and put it in her pocket. "For my box of mementos," she said.

The wedding dress was another matter. Tradition decreed that it was the bride's family who had to pay for it. "Ask Jack's mother for a good address," Pearl's mother told her. "She must know of a Jewish shop where you can buy a wedding dress cheap."

So Pearl asked Nesha, who gave her the address of a Jewish-owned shop in Brighton, on the cheap end of downtown, and a whole family delegation went downtown together to select the wedding dress: Pearl, her mother, and her grandmother Henrietta. Pearl had insisted on bringing her grandmother—who rarely went out nowadays—to make it seem like more of a ceremony. Despite the bare-bones look of the shop, it held a decent assortment of dresses.

* * *

Pearl swirled about in the dress, and the world dropped away. The shame of shopping for a bargain dress, when her father could easily have afforded a better one, no longer mattered. Today was the very last time in her life that she would have to pinch pennies. Jack would pay for her dresses now. She basked in the thought of what this meant: a green sequined gown she had seen in a shop window, a fox fur stole. She would be beautiful, and he would adore her.

She felt beautiful right now, in the heavenly dress that had been somehow conjured up from the unpromising little shop. Today was her day, even more than the wedding day would be. For on the wedding day she would have to deal with Jack's odd family, and the tactless remarks her father was sure to make about them, and Jack's tension about his father's demands about how the ceremony must be arranged. Today, she was on top of the world.

* * *

Henrietta must have been asleep and dreaming, for suddenly the shop was gone, and it was her own wedding day. She saw herself from a distance, young and beautiful in her wedding dress, but it was a modern dress, nothing like the one she had actually worn more than fifty years ago.

"Grandmother, are you all right?" Right in front of her was her granddaughter trying on a dress. Now which granddaughter was she? And what was it she'd said about the groom? A black-haired young immigrant boy from a wealthy family. "You know the family," some-

one had said. But how could that be? It was all so muddled up in her mind. When the pinning was completed, Pearl quickly removed the dress and reached for her grandmother's hand. "I'll get you right home, Grandmother," she said.

Henrietta took the arm gratefully. She held her head up high, and politely told the worried-looking young girl how much she had enjoyed the outing. Though once she was safely inside her home, she could not say where she had been, or whether she'd dreamed the whole thing.

* * *

Wedding day: August 29, 1909.

It was supposed to be the most beautiful day of a young woman's life. Pearl knew she looked ravishing in her dress, but when Jake arrived for her in the carriage, he scarcely looked at her. She pouted. "Are you so afraid of that big bad bear, your father?"

Jake nodded tensely. His ears were still ringing from the lecture he had received the previous evening. Behr had laid down the law in no uncertain terms. "You've been very disrespectful," he said, "but you were a bachelor and there's leeway. Now you're the head of a household in the eyes of your family, your community, and the Jews who trust the name Manischewitz." What had followed was a list of restrictions on their future life that he would have to tell her about very soon.

"Well dear, it will be over soon, won't it?" Pearl kissed his cheek reassuringly.

And indeed, the ceremony in the cool, dim study of the Orthodox rabbi was short. Pearl understood very little of it, but when the rabbi placed the Jewish marriage certificate on the table, she was awed by the beautifully hand-colored document, printed in Budapest. *What a treasure*, she thought. After the signing, they were released into the sunlit street where their carriage was waiting to bring them to the Odd Fellows Temple. The second ceremony at the Odd Fellows Temple was short too. But the words went right to Pearl's heart when Jake said them in English, with all the passion in his soul: "Behold, you are consecrated to me with this ring, according to the Law of Moses and Israel."

Then the family and guests sat down for the wedding dinner, a kosher feast, probably the first ever served in that irreverent building. The pious group in black coats contrasted weirdly with Lee's modern American family sitting opposite them, but the abundant, delicious food bridged the gap admirably.

At the end of the meal, Pearl walked over to Nesha. She squeezed her mother-in-law's hand and said, "Mama, thank you for everything," in a way that assured Nesha her letter had been understood and taken to heart. The marriage would be safe.

* * *

Pearl and Jake took a honeymoon trip to Cambridge Springs, Pennsylvania, where they spent three weeks feasting on love.

On the last day they talked about their future life as a married couple. Jake tried to keep the tone light.

"Sweetheart, on the Jewish holidays we can't go out on the town anymore. We'll just close the curtains and then—watch out." He winked playfully.

"You naughty boy." Pearl kissed his cheek. "Out with it—I know there is more. What else mustn't we do?"

Jake took a deep breath. "No seafood. Ever. And you'll have to buy all our meat from Oscherwitz." Behr's friend Oscherowitz had dropped an *o* from his name and expanded his business nicely, with the result that one of his butcher shops was not far from the young couple's new apartment at Eighth and Lynn Streets.

"Whether you want to prepare the meat according to Jewish law once you bring it home is up to your own conscience. Mama says she'll help you if you like."

Pearl did not reply right away. She allowed herself the pleasure of seeing him wait anxiously for her answer.

Jake and Pearl on their honeymoon, August 1909.

"Yes, darling, I will be your obedient little wifey." She said it with a little pout. The pout excited him, and soon they were kissing, and the serious talk was ended.

At least she had agreed; Jake was nearly sure of it, and he would tell Mama, so that she too could be relieved. The family would keep a united front.

But for how long?

Chapter 6

For He Has Dealt Kindly

*Return, my soul, to your rest, for the Lord has dealt kindly
with you. For You have delivered my soul from death, my
eyes from tears, my foot from stumbling.*
        —Psalm 116 (from the Passover Haggadah)

Why were the other women so jealous of her? Nesha tried to be
friendly with everyone. Some of the women looked at her so
meanly that she was afraid they might bring on the evil eye.

At the meeting of the Benevolent Society, she asked a woman
she knew—her name was Pera Gittel Touff—how her son Harry
was doing these days, such a fine scholar and God-fearing young
man. The woman practically snorted at her before answering,
"Just fine, thank God." Whatever had Nesha done to offend her?

The woman named Pera Gittel fled to the women's toilet at the
rear of the synagogue and scrutinized her face in the small mirror. She tucked a few strands of stringy gray hair under her hat.
Pera Gittel's thoughts were bitter.

*"How is my son Harry?" Huh! He'd be fine if he had a decent start
in life. And if I'd come to America with a healthy young husband as
Nesha Manischewitz did, I guess I could wear fine silk dresses and
ridiculous hats as she does. But no, my Goetzel had to wait until he
was forty-eight and we were nearly starving in Lithuania before he
picked himself up and got on a boat.*

And then what? Then my Harry had to stay behind and finish his religious studies. Now Harry's a fine scholar, and Behr Manischewitz himself comes to see my son in his miserable little apartment, and listens to my son's opinions. But does Behr Manischewitz help my son to find a job? No, and worse, he fills my son's head with nonsense. "Don't make a living from Torah" he says, when my son applies for a decent job teaching. And from what should a man make a living, I ask you, when all he knows is Torah?

* * *

Four children married, God bless them all. Nesha was proud of them. And Behr's matzo business still growing bigger, and grandchildren on the way. But almost before this lovely picture was painted, there were cracks in it. Had she and Behr had done something to attract the evil eye? The thought made a shiver go right down her back.

For a while now, she had seen signs that her husband was no longer healthy. Signs that would not be noticed by anyone else. The photograph, for instance.

"I've made an appointment for us at the photographers tomorrow," Behr said one evening. "See that my best coat is ready."

She felt her hands go clammy. Behr had seldom agreed to have his photograph taken. Some rabbis were against photography because of the biblical injunction against making graven images. But others said the interdiction did not apply. Probably Behr had considered photographs frivolous, like birthday parties or parlor games.

There was nothing frivolous about this trip to the photographer.

"What a fine idea," she said.

What else could she say? That she knew he was thinking of death? That she knew he wanted a photograph for his sons to keep after he was dead, and for the world to remember him by?

The next morning she laid out the suit for him. When he was ready to leave, she smoothed the lapel gently, patted the collar, and then let her hand linger over the whole broad width of his back, eliminating the smallest wrinkle. He gave her a surprised look. Embarrassed, she dropped her hand to her side.

In the photograph, Behr's compelling eyes look straight out at the viewer. His mustache and beard are perfectly groomed. His broad, high forehead looks smooth and untroubled under the elegant black skullcap, even at fifty-four. Nobody but the man's wife could guess at the somber thoughts behind that smooth forehead.

* * *

Portrait of Behr at age 54.

Behr continued to work as hard as ever. He continued his charitable activities too. For this he rarely took time away from his work, but instead worked late in the evening. He persisted even though a solution was right at hand—his son Jake.

In 1910, the annual baking of matzo began on the first of November. The starting date of the matzo-baking season had been moved up earlier each year as sales increased.

Before the baking season started, the ovens had to be dismantled for cleaning and then reassembled. Jake loved this operation every bit as much as his father did—and it was a job for a younger man.

But Behr kept sending him on business trips, and handled the most stressful work in the matzo factory himself. "You should give Jake the hard work at the factory, it's too much for you," Nesha said, "Instead of sending him out on the road."

She had finally learned to speak her mind to Behr, and he no longer exploded when she did. But this new liberty, once taken, turned out to be next to useless, since he ignored her advice anyway.

So Jake did the traveling: one week in Philadelphia, and the next week in New York, Boston, or Baltimore. He wrote his young wife almost daily letters, in hotels and even when on the train. She showed one of them to Nesha.

> On train to New York, noontime,
> October 23, 1910
> My Most Beloved Pearl,
> I sincerely hope you are not feeling hard toward me for neglecting you as much as I have. Really dear, this trip has been about the hardest I have yet had to tackle, and to make matters still worse, it seems to have been almost entirely fruitless. As for my feelings for you—well—I can only say that I certainly don't want to go through this again! Missed you! Hell, just YOU WAIT and see when I come back to you and

judge for yourself! From the outlook just now, I expect to leave New York Wednesday night on that fastest Penn train and be home to you on Thursday morning, and if you really love me then you must meet me without fail. I surely hope this will find you well and happy and the same for all of our dear ones. Give them all a sweet kiss for me, especially Mother.

With my deepest Love and Admiration and my most sincere Loyalty and Devotion to you,
I am for ever your Jack

"How sweet," said Nesha. She read through the letter a second and a third time. "So different from his father!" It was a remark that she could not have formulated a few years earlier. Ever since Jake had given her a glimpse of his passion for Pearl, she knew that other husbands might be different from her own.

Pearl laughed naughtily. "Perhaps they're not so different after all, Mother."

Nesha looked at her blankly, then reddened as she realized what Pearl meant. Jake was eager to get back to his wife and into her bed, just as Behr always was.

Pearl acted innocent. "Well, they both love their work, don't they?"

She put the letter away carefully in her velvet-lined box.

Pearl gave birth to a son, Howard, a year and a half after the wedding, in March 1911. The matzo ovens were going full force, day and night.

During those pre-Passover weeks, torn between two passions, Jake often paused in the afternoon to dash off a letter to Pearl. He wrote on the company stationery, while the office messenger boy stood by, waiting to hand-deliver the letter.

My Darling Pearl,
I believe you will at once understand that the mission of

this note is to say that I cannot see you today. Let me know if you are really feeling well today. I must insist on an answer from you to the delivery boy, For if not, then I will make it my business to see you this evening. But if you are well, which I hope that you are! then I feel that my importance in the business warrants my ever-present attention for today.

　　With my sincere Love and Kisses, I am ever your loving and devoted
Jack

When the messenger returned with Pearl's assurance that all was well, he turned his attention back to the ovens, his face flushed and excited, just as his father's was, and the two worked side by side late into the night.

But the relationship between father and son was as stormy as ever.

Jake appeared at his mother's door in the middle of a bright May afternoon.

"Mother, I can't take it from Father any longer, I've quit!"

He paced around the living room, trying to put his frustration into words. Father's insistence over what might be, but wasn't really, a point of Jewish law. Father's autocratic tones. Father's, well, just everything! And then he stormed out again, to disappear for the rest of the day.

Nesha was left standing helplessly in the front hall.

After a few minutes she recovered. She pulled on a light spring coat and headed downtown to her son's apartment. She arrived breathless, to find Pearl reading tranquilly by the window, while the baby napped and the housemaid ironed.

Pearl laughed, a long, deep-throated laugh, when she heard Nesha's story.

"Has he quit again? He'll be at work tomorrow morning at seven, Mother. He must break loose some days, you know."

She patted Nesha's knee reassuringly.

"The first time was so long ago. He came to find me in the recess break, when I was still in school. He said, 'Hell, Pearl, I can't take it with Father any more,' and all my girlfriends wanted to know what had happened. The next day it was all forgotten; he wouldn't even mention it. He loves his work, Mother. And he loves Father, too, in spite of everything."

He was back at work the next morning.

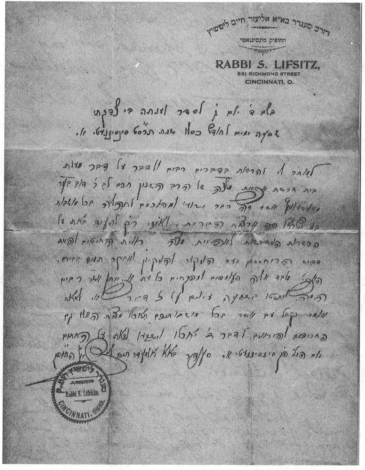

Hechsher letter from Rabbi Lifshitz certifying kashrut, 1911.

But Behr was still not ready to hand over responsibility for the factory to Jake. In June, when Jake's baby was just three months old, Behr sent Jake off to Toronto. Behr did not exactly say he was thinking of building a factory there, but he allowed the rumor to circulate.

"Labor's cheaper in Canada," he said, when Nesha asked whether that was his intention. "Jake can look into it."

Jake rented an apartment for a few months and moved his family to Toronto. He could not bear to be without Pearl for so long.

Pearl made the best of life in Canada. She wrote to all her family and friends to please come and visit her and the baby, while Jake made all the additional side trips his father deemed necessary. In June he made a trip to Buffalo, and in July he was in Boston.

In July Nesha went as usual to take the waters at Mount Clemens. She had begun to pin the most unrealistic hopes on her annual cure at the baths. Could it somehow heal her aching abdomen? The pains were sharper and more persistent lately. She didn't discuss this with her doctor, for it embarrassed her. In any case, the bath cure was probably all that modern science could offer.

When she returned home, Pearl and the baby were still in Canada, and Jake was off making another side trip to Buffalo. Finally, in October—just before the matzo-baking season began—the exiled family was allowed to move back to Cincinnati. Nothing came of the idea of a factory in Canada, but matzo sales there increased. Sales were increasing all the time anyway.

In January, Jake was off to Chicago. And so it went—1912 was a year of travel for Jake.

* * *

In 1913, Behr planned to move the bakery to yet another site, on West Eighth Street. "It's going to be the largest matzo factory in the world," he told Nesha. He was going to install a new machine for packing the matzo in boxes.

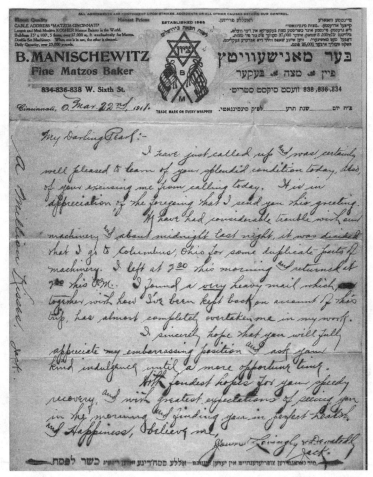

Letter from Jake to Pearl on company stationery (1911).

"With my new packing machine, God willing, I'll be able to deliver matzos all over the world, wherever there are Jews," he said.

"God willing, your health will hold up, with so much hard work." She shook her head doubtfully.

"God willing."

Behr continued his frequent visits to the Milling Machine Company. He had continued patenting his more important equipment. The most important patent had been the "traveling-carrier bake-oven," a conveyor-belt system whereby the dough was placed on one end and slowly moved through the oven chambers.

On his way to the Milling Machine Company, Behr usually stopped at the home of one of his friends, a young man named Harry Touff. How he enjoyed these visits! Harry did not have a clue about the nuts-and-bolts questions of factory equipment. He was an unworldly young man, just like the boys who had been Behr's classmates long ago in Telz. And small wonder in that – Harry had sat on those same benches, some twenty years after Behr had completed his studies and moved on. Talking to Harry gave Behr some rare moments of relaxation. Plus, their conversations together were laced with Talmudic references, a special habit of speech that could not be used with everyone. Clearly Harry had been a top student in his class at the yeshiva, just like Behr.

* * *

His friend Harry. This was another ominous sign, if anything was. Why should her husband suddenly need this new friendship?

The friendship had begun almost the day the young man arrived in Cincinnati. Harry had studied at the same yeshiva in Telz where Behr had studied. He'd arrived at about nineteen, right after finishing his studies.

What was so special about the young man? Nesha asked her husband this question, and his answer was razor-sharp.

"The young man is a Talmudic scholar—you won't find another young man like him in all of Cincinnati. And his father is one of the best scholars here, maybe even the best. Long life to them both!"

Nesha said no more. But she resented Harry's intrusion into her husband's life. There was a house of study downtown where Behr could study any evening of the week with men his own age, as he always used to do. At the young man's apartment, she was sure they just drank tea and did not discuss Talmud. Harry lived down on Central Avenue in a small apartment with his wife and little girls, over his wife's shop. Hardly an atmosphere for discussing Talmud!

It wasn't so hard to get to the heart of the matter: Harry was the sort of young man Behr would have wanted as a son. Like his brother's son, the one named Jacob, who had studied at the yeshiva in Telz, who still lived in Telz today, most likely. Behr no longer spoke of the nephew in Telz. How old would he be now? Nesha wondered. Just a little older than her own son Jake.

After an afternoon with Harry, Behr's bitterness was sure to come out in an angry flare-up with Jake. There was always something to blame his son for, when Behr came back from Harry's. Every word Behr said in praise of his young friend was a poisoned arrow aimed directly at Jake.

Jake must hate that young man, she thought. *And—God forgive me—I think I hate him too.*

* * *

"You might come with me to the spa," Nesha suggested to her husband. It was June 1913, and Behr's health was declining more obviously now.

"It might be good for you—the water."

Her own pains were getting still worse, and last year's cure hadn't helped much. But there was nothing better. And her husband looked so pale—was he having pains too?

The visits to his friend Harry became more frequent.

* * *

The next unpleasant development was Behr's moodiness. He began to mull aloud over what would become of his family after his death. Nesha dreaded these conversations.

Meyer, their oldest son, was still single at thirty. Behr saw this as a willful act, the sinister culmination of his son's disobedience.

"Meyer will never have children, and you can be sure that I won't have him take my place in the matzo business either," he told Nesha. His face twisted in bitterness. "You know what's in my will!"

"Yes, I know." She sighed. He had decided that Jake would inherit the lion's share of the company and take over the reins. But this was no reason for anger. Each son was different.

Their third son, Joseph, had been married in January, but Behr's mood hadn't improved. He seemed to focus only on his disappointments.

When he spoke of his fourth son, Max, it was in the same bitter tones he used for Meyer. What rankled him was that, even though Max's bride Edith had been chosen from a very pious family, the couple had been married for six years now and was still childless.

"Maybe they spite the will of God and intervene to prevent a childbirth, doing the work of the Evil One, God forbid!"

Nesha was left speechless.

She knew that such awful things were possible. Pearl had taken charge of Nesha's belated education in the ways of the world, and told her about abortions. The free, modern life had its ugly underside. It wasn't just a matter of young women enjoying ice cream parlors and going to Coney Island with young men.

But her son Max and his wife Edith from the Holy Land wouldn't do such a thing. They hadn't thrown off the yoke of religion, though they had other interests too. In fact, they were active in the religious community. Later (though Behr would not live to see this), Max would become president of the Hebrew schools.

Cautiously, Nesha reassured her husband.

"Max and Edith are God-fearing," she said.

By this she meant that the couple was simply unable to have children, which was God's will, not a subject for anger. Behr grunted.

"And Mayme has given you two fine grandchildren in New York, may the evil eye not learn about it."

She avoided counting the grandchildren on her fingers, for that was unlucky. But there were, thank God, already enough to count:

"And you have Hirsh's two precious little ones in Jerusalem, and Jake's precious little Howard. And Hirsh's Sarah and our Pearl are both expecting again, God bless them both."

Behr refused to be cheered.

"Jake's son," he said, and his voice was ominous. "What do I know about Jake and his sons? In thirty years, God forbid, they may all be Gentiles. All intermarried and converted. A son begins with disobedience and, God forbid, it ends in catastrophe; such things happen!"

Nesha could find no reply to this. How could he think such a thing was likely? Jake was respectful of the traditions, at least outwardly. On Sabbaths and on Jewish holidays, he and Pearl stayed quietly at home or went to the park; they were not seen desecrating the tradition. But it was not enough for Behr.

"Nothing good can come of breaking the yoke of Torah," he said.

Nothing good can come of spreading bitterness either.

Nesha nearly said this out loud. But it would only have made him continue his outburst, so she bit her tongue and waited for him to calm himself.

* * *

By the year's end, Behr's mood was totally unpredictable. He was quick to anger, and quick to assume the worst.

On one day late in December 1913, Behr went to Jake's apartment for a visit. Pearl had given birth to her second son, Bernard, just a couple of days earlier, on Christmas Eve.

When Behr arrived, he took in the scene at a glance. Gift-wrapping paper was spread about in disorder on the floor. Two-year-old Howard was playing merrily with a wooden horse that had obviously just come out of a gift package. On the mantelpiece stood a small array of Christmas greeting cards.

Behr was furious at what he mistakenly thought was a Christmas celebration.

"What's this celebration I see!" he shouted.

"It has nothing to do with Christmas, Father," said Pearl. She spoke respectfully, although she was close to tears.

The gifts were for the new baby. And little Howard had received a few consolation gifts, so that he wouldn't be jealous.

At last Behr understood his error and calmed down. He allowed himself to be served tea by the young housemaid, who was waiting uncertainly in the kitchen.

"It isn't good for your health, Father, to excite yourself so," Pearl said. She looked pale and tired in her silk dressing gown. Jake stood stiffly by the fireplace, holding in his anger at his father.

After Behr left, the young couple had one of their rare quarrels.

"Darling, you have to admit that things would have gone better if you'd put away the Christmas cards."

Jake said this in what he thought was a tone of fond reproach, and he nearly got away with it. But he could not resist adding one fatal remark.

"And the New Year's card with the cupid on it, from your sister Stella—you have to admit it was a bit too much!"

And at that, Pearl—who was very tired and weak, as well she might be—replied with a few remarks about her father-in-law that were not particularly complimentary.

And then Jake replied a little too hotly, and very soon Pearl was crying and Jake had to kiss her and apologize.

It was the last such incident, for Behr did not live many months longer. He died in March 1914, at age fifty-seven, after a short illness.

* * *

Rabbis and representatives from Jewish societies within a radius of a thousand miles attended Behr's funeral. Among the many local groups that were represented was a large official delegation from the Zionist Society of Cincinnati.

Jake never left his mother's side. He bore with the long prayers, the endless presence of numerous pious bearded men in long black coats, with full head covering (black hats over black *yarmulkes*). He shook hands patiently with each and every one of them, and nodded at the long Hebrew phrases that he knew were words of condolence, but that reminded him maddeningly of his interminable days in the Talmud Torah.

Man, oh man, what a grim way to go, he thought, as the prayers droned on. *Pearl's old man said he aims to go off with a marching band. That's what they do in the Rotary Club. What would the rabbis say if I told them that's how I want to go?*

There's Harry now, Father's pet, looking all pale and pained as if he'd lost his best friend. At least Harry's clean-shaven now, so maybe he's not so pious as Father made him out to be. People say he shaved his beard off in order to apply for a job teaching Talmud at the Hebrew Union College, where they teach the clean-shaven pseudo-rabbis. But he didn't get the job anyway. I wager Father wouldn't have been so stuck on him if he'd known about that escapade.

He took his mother's arm and gave it a little encouraging squeeze. This was for Mama, after all. How was she taking it? He kept an anxious eye on her until at last they were safely home.

During the days of mourning, Jake stayed close to his mother, and so did Pearl. Nesha was surrounded by family, friends, and acquaintances. There wasn't much time for her to examine her own feelings, nor would she have wanted to. She'd been prepared for Behr's death, and she'd been very patient with him in the past few months. She wasn't afraid of any reproach from heaven on his account. It was time to think of her sons and their future.

As soon as letters could be exchanged with Jerusalem, Hirsh announced his plans for a trip home.

"I shall arrive in Cincinnati in July, God willing," he wrote, "with my wife and our three children, long life to them. It is my sincere wish, dear Mother, to be some consolation to you."

Hirsh had just turned twenty-three in April. His second wife, Sarah, had already given birth to two children. But events in Jerusalem had only barely touched Nesha's consciousness over the past five years. Now here was this faraway young man—almost a stranger—saying he wanted to be a consolation to her.

Hirsh sent a telegram when he landed in New York. When he arrived with his wife and children at the Cincinnati station, Jake and Pearl were there to meet them.

The two brothers greeted each other stiffly.

Jake hadn't seen his younger brother for fourteen years. There had been no contact between the brothers in all this time. Behr had carried on a correspondence in Hebrew with his son in Palestine. But he had shared none of this with Jake, who usually kept conversations with his father safely focused on the matzo business.

So the young man that Jake brought home from the train station and deposited in his mother's parlor was a stranger.

It was Nesha's task to welcome her rail-thin young daughter-in-law Sarah into the family. The young woman seemed so fragile, it was hard to believe she had given birth to two children, and that she was also caring for her husband's motherless older son, Joshua. Sarah sat rigidly in Nesha's parlor and self-consciously straightened her skirt and headscarf.

"Are you hungry? Can I get you something?" Nesha said in Yiddish.

Her daughter-in-law did not answer immediately. Had she understood? Nesha wondered suddenly whether her Yiddish had changed a lot over the years in America.

Little Joshua's shrill voice broke the silence. "Mama, is there something to drink in America?"

The two women laughed, and the ice was broken. Nesha brought him a syrupy American drink that was evidently new to him, and the little boy laughed out loud in surprise.

Then the atmosphere began to relax. Nesha asked the young woman to tell about her journey. As she listened, her thoughts drifted.

How foreign they were, this young couple from Palestine! *Was I also so young and awkward when I arrived in America? I feel more comfortable with Pearl and Jake than with this strange couple.* It was a lifetime ago that she had arrived with her husband and three little children. A quarter of a century. She too hadn't known a word of English.

Where had the years gone?

What was left for her in the years that remained to her? Only to help her sons on their way, to make sure they were starting out right.

Hirsh announced his plans at the dinner table. He spoke in Yiddish.

"I don't mean to stay here long. God willing, we will be going back to Palestine very soon. I only want to be with Mother for a while and wait until our inheritance from Father has been settled."

"Which of those things would you say is the more essential?" Jake growled in English. His brother did not reply, but continued in Yiddish.

"I shall continue to study, and to support my family by managing the orange groves which Father bought for us there."

"Orange groves? What's this about orange groves?" There was a dangerous tone to Jake's voice that threatened to break the peace of the evening.

"Of course you will," Nesha said quickly, hoping in this way to signal to Jake that she knew about the orange groves and would explain to him later.

She turned to Hirsh.

"Your father, may he rest in peace, got a lot of satisfaction from that purchase. He wanted to have the honor of a purchase of land in Palestine, and to provide you with a livelihood so you could study. God willing, you should enjoy."

"May I have some more dessert?" asked Joshua. Nesha took his bowl to be filled, and the subject was closed.

The next day Jake went over his father's account books to see exactly what had been purchased for Hirsh. The price in dollars had not been high. Jake was mollified.

The very next week the World War began. Hirsh and his family would never return to live in Palestine. The orange groves would be confiscated during the war. Hirsh would remain in Cincinnati to work in the matzo factory along with his brothers.

Nesha took Sarah under her wing the following Monday. The two women sat in the kitchen, with the children underfoot.

"When I first arrived I didn't know a word of English either," she said. "A kind woman named Henrietta helped me know what to do, for instance about the schools."

Sarah listened attentively. Nesha continued.

"The older boy can go straight to school and learn English," she said. "I will take you there tomorrow. And the children will need English names, to use at school."

"I intend to learn to read and write English myself, just as soon as I can!"

Nesha was surprised at the shrill, determined voice coming from this diminutive young woman.

She already knew the young woman's story. Sarah had been a toddler when her young father somehow drowned in a well in

Jerusalem. A second husband had been found for Sarah's eighteen-year-old widowed mother. But the new husband, a rabbi, had refused to allow his bride to bring her orphaned children into her new home. Little Sarah and her infant brother were sent to separate homes, where there were already many children and little money or love to spare. Sarah was put to work sewing as soon as her small hands were skillful enough to hold a needle. And at sixteen a match was made for her with the young widower Hirsh, and Hirsh's motherless baby son was put in her hands.

Frail-looking Sarah was actually made of steel. She would find her place in the Orthodox community, learn English, and play an active role in a whole array of charities, in Cincinnati and then in New York, for many, many years. And she would live to be a hundred and two.

Nesha's main concern now was to see that her sons got off to the right start together.

She and Jake already knew the contents of Behr's will, and Hirsh was soon informed. In his last testament, Behr had tried to maintain his influence over the family even after death. He had set out stipulations to ensure the success of the business for the next generation, and to protect them from any rash decisions they might make through inexperience.

His first stipulation was that the business was to become a corporation, and was to be named The B. Manischewitz Company. Jake received the largest inheritance, five percent more than each of his brothers, and would head his father's business as president of the new corporation.

The will further stipulated that the sons who were not yet married would only receive their inheritance on condition that they married Orthodox women. This condition only concerned Meyer, for the others were married. Nesha was well provided for with an annual sum from the earnings of the stock dividends. No stock would be offered for sale. Each daughter would receive a generous sum of money, but no part in the family business. The younger daughters would not receive their portion until they were married to Orthodox husbands. Ten percent of the stock would be held by trustees as a charitable trust, and the trustees would select charities to benefit from the dividends, of which more than half had to be in the Holy Land. A bequest of three thousand dollars was left to the Cincinnati Talmud Torah, the school that Behr had helped to found many years before.

Notice of the company's incorporation was to be printed on a card, one side in English, one side in Yiddish, with assurance that the company guaranteed its continued adherence to "principles of commercial honor and strict observance of the Jewish law."

Behr had thought of everything. Except one thing: would his sons be able to carry out his plans?

No two brothers were close to each other, not even the ones who were close in age and had grown up in America. Each had gone his own way. "It's the American way," Nesha used to say with a little sigh.

But she knew she was lying to herself. Behr's strictness had scattered his sons. Each boy had felt that it was safest to keep to himself, in order to keep out of his father's path. The two boys who grew up in Palestine didn't have much in common with one another either. Hirsh was the pious son Behr had dreamed of. His brother Max had a completely different way of life.

It wasn't much of a group to carry on a business together.

She tried to explain this to Jake that same week.

"Jake, it's going to be your job to keep your brothers together, or you won't have any business left in a few years. You can't let your feelings lead you astray."

The first time she said it, Jake said nothing. But she knew he would think about it.

She repeated her advice to Jake more than once in the following weeks. And she thought about it a lot. The brothers had been given positions in the company under Behr's will: Hirsh and Meyer were vice-presidents, Joseph was secretary, Max was treasurer. But relationships were more than a set of titles.

First, there was the problem of Meyer, the oldest. He did not seem too resentful of Jake's superior position, but you never could never know for sure. Like many men, he seldom spoke about his feelings. Nesha had a little talk with Meyer about his interests and learned that he felt Cincinnati was too small for him.

"Jake, there is something that you can do for your brother Meyer."

Jake raised his eyebrows. What could he do for Meyer?

". . . and it will be very good for the company, too. You can let him be in charge of sales and distribution in New York."

Jake considered this, and wondered why he hadn't thought of it himself. New York was the biggest market—his brother would have plenty of work. Anyway, New York was getting to be a sort of second pole for the family. Mayme had remained in New York after her marriage and had invited her younger sisters to visit her there. One of them, Rose, had married there in May, almost as soon as she knew the conditions of her father's will.

Meyer packed his bags and left for New York as soon as Jake told him about it.

The question of Hirsh's role in the company was much more critical. A few weeks later, Nesha told Jake her plan.

"Jake, you have to let Hirsh play more of a role in the company. You want people to know the bakery can still be trusted to be as kosher as it was with your father."

"Trusted! By God, Mother, you think I can't be trusted? I have the factory inspected at least as often as Father did. It's one hundred percent kosher, and you know it!"

"I know it, my son, but the Jews who buy, they also have to know it. Your brother goes out there in the community, he makes a nice impression, you should both live to a hundred and twenty. You have to let him represent us when there are occasions, charities, everything like that. You see what I mean?"

Yes, he saw what she meant. And he didn't like it.

"Why did I ever get into this?" he exclaimed. "Did I ask to have a business where religion is always hanging over me?"

He fumed about it throughout the month of August.

In September, Jake received an invitation from the Talmud Torah Society, to attend a special meeting in honor of the generous gift received from the Manischewitz family in Behr's will.

Jake read it several times, feeling frustration welling up in him. *Damn, this is one of those occasions Mama was talking about.* Dealing with the Talmud Torah always made him feel like a rebellious boy seated in a classroom. His mother was right—it would look better for a religious member of the family to attend.

Jake replied to the Talmud Torah Society, excusing himself on the grounds of "a slight indisposition," and told them that his brother Hirsh would attend in his place, accompanied by their mother.

Nesha attended the ceremony proudly with her Jerusalem-educated son at her side. The president of the Committee for the Talmud Torah Society read out the paragraph of Behr's will stipulating the conditions of the grant, and said a great many good things about her husband. Hirsh said a few words that were exactly right for the occasion, and he shook many hands and made just the right impression on everybody. He remained close to his mother's side all the while. She had been tired when she arrived, but she revived completely before the ceremony ended. It was the first of hundreds of occasions where Hirsh would represent the Manischewitz family.

She went home feeling good about her husband, about her sons, and about herself.

In September Meyer was married in New York. His wife, Minn, was a young woman from a religious family.

"So Meyer, too, wants to be sure of his inheritance!" Jake remarked, in acid tones. Quite a few other people who knew about Behr's will made the same remark.

But Meyer and Minn, who never had children, remained together for many years, and they may have married for love, for who can say for sure?

The unveiling of Behr's tombstone was held in November. This time Nesha had not just one but four of her sons with her at the cemetery of the Lithuanian Jewish community on the barren, windy hilltop of Price Hill. The tall tombstone was engraved with a Hebrew inscription that formed an anagram in which the first letter of each line spelled out Behr's name. The rabbi read it out loud.

Distinguished among ten thousand, and a man among men
He found a grave for himself here in the best of graves
Alas, it is grievous for mother and children
Nothing remains for them but sighs all their days
Incomplete and short was his life, but great were his works
Schooled in charity and shining in generosity,
He engaged in study of Torah and knowledge
Which he bequeathed to his offspring to observe
Indeed the heavens on high will tell
What this righteous man for all ages has accomplished

The date was inscribed beneath the poem in Hebrew. Below it was the name Manischewitz in English. It was the only English word on the tombstone.

"Father's name meant so much to him, may he rest in peace!" said Jake. He was holding his mother's arm.

"And to all of us," said Nesha.

With a son on each side of her, she left the cemetery.

The unveiling of the tombstone was the last social occasion that Nesha attended. She began to have more frequent pains in her abdomen, and spent more time consulting doctors and resting in bed.

Jake came to see her daily, of course. And her beloved Pearl came often, sometimes with her little boys. Hirsh came to visit her each week, with his wife and their children. Joseph also had a son now, and came to visit her with his family. And Max came too, though he would soon be moving to New York, to be out of Jake's way, like Meyer.

At least they were all getting along together, well enough to keep the family livelihood secure. She could stop worrying about that and leave it to Jake. He was on the right track now. If only he would not worry so much about her. All through the year of her husband's death, and the next year, he made daily visits. "Mama, are you feeling better?" he always asked, taking her hand in hers and giving her such an anxious look that it was hard to tell the truth, and she had to say, "Well, maybe just a tiny bit better."

In fact it was a struggle for her just to get through the day and seat herself in the least painful position to await her son's visit in the evening. She allowed the housemaid to do everything for her, even the cooking.

She usually remained seated, to avoid the pains that could strike her when she strained herself. She let the housemaid serve the tea.

On Sabbath afternoons she spent hours sitting on the porch, if the weather was warm enough, with her dog-eared copy of the Book of Psalms on her lap, eating her favorite pineapple candies, the same ones that Jake had first brought her when he was a little boy. There were always some of the grandchildren around.

Who would have believed that one day she would just sit and let others come to her? "The children will remember me as a fine lady," she told Jake, trying to lighten her tone for his sake. "Just sitting here and letting everyone take care of me.

It was May, 1916, and the evening breeze was soft and gentle, wafting the curtain in the living room where Jake sat opposite his mother, anxiously watching her. She could see a new wrinkle line in his forehead. "Sometimes it's best to just accept God's plan," she said softly, and this was as close as they came to speaking of her death. He nearly crushed her hand as he replied, "I'll always love you, Mama."

A few days later, she was in bed when Jake arrived in the spring twilight. "Was the doctor here?" he said in a strangled voice that wanted nothing more than an enemy to accuse. Nesha shook her head, and the doctor was called immediately, and came that same evening. The doctor bustled about, and recommended a potion, but a certain edge to his voice made it clear that there was nothing in his bag of tricks to heal his patient. And the next evening, and the next, she was in bed when her dear son arrived, and the candies he brought her remained on her night table untouched.

She grew weaker each day, faster now, and her son's misery grew, as did his anger at the doctor, whenever the man was unlucky enough to still be in the house upon his arrival. But all the son's despair could not keep his mother from slipping away from him, and before the summer arrived, she was gone.

Jake, Pearl, Bernard and Howard – family portrait, 1917.

Chapter 7

Acceptable in Thy Sight

Ended the act of the Pesach night

Each law and custom kept aright:

As we've lived to do it without a stain,

God grant we do it time and again.

— *Passover Haggadah*

Mama would be proud to see how well I'm doing. Jake hummed a monotonous tune to himself as he climbed the slope to the Lithuanian Jewish Cemetery. The thought made him feel a little better, after a hectic streetcar ride and a wobbly ascent by the inclined railway up to the windswept hilltop. It was always blustery up on Price Hill, and his heavy coat and fashionable black silk scarf did not seem to be much help.

Jake hated cemeteries. But it was autumn already, and he felt the pull of it, the need to visit Mama's grave again. He missed Mama every day, and by God, a man could grieve anywhere—but sometimes he felt he needed to be there, at her graveside, especially in autumn with all the leaves falling. It was 1918 now, two years and three months since she had died.

As if seeking reassurance, he felt around in his pocket for his business cards. *Mama would love my new cards,* he thought: Jacob Manischewitz, president of the B. Manischewitz Company.

The factory on Eighth Street, Cincinnati .

The factory in downtown Cincinnati, the one his father had dreamed of completing at the time of his death, was now the biggest matzo bakery in the world. This was what the full-page advertisements in the *Israelite* said at Passover time. Another thing that Mama would have loved to see. But she'd only lived for two years after Father.

He'd reached the grave now, and as always the freshly carved date was what hit him in the face: 17 Sivan 5677. June 1916. *Way too early*. Mama had been sick for years and nobody gave a damn. She'd gone to the spa each year until she was in too much pain to go there. He should sue those crooks for quackery with their putrid water. Afterwards she'd just parked herself at home. Everyone had been nice to her at the end, but only Jake knew how she'd suffered. For everyone else, Mama was the drudge who had just obeyed Father till he was no longer there.

Jake stood motionless and studied the two gravestones. The name Manischewitz was the only word in English on them, in big letters. Mama was proud of the verse on Father's grave, written so that the first letters of each line spelled his name. Now a matching column of Hebrew verses stood on her own grave: she'd have liked that, too. But the praise of her on it was so stilted, so different from his warmhearted, sometimes silly, but ever-loving Mama:

"She sent her sons to Jerusalem, To learn Torah there," the inscription read. *As if that was the thing Mama should be most proud of. She was prouder of me for not leaving her.* But gravestones weren't supposed to be honest, were they?

Jake looked around. Stretching out below him was a large empty field. You could tell it was meant to be filled with the graves of people who were this very moment going about their business down in the city, unaware of the place that awaited them here. Already Father's row had been nearly filled. The father of that annoying Harry, Father's pet—a much older man than Father—had died recently and was buried just two graves farther down the row.

"We all have to go sometime," he said aloud. But why did some go sooner than others?

He said no formal prayer, because he was alone, and religion was a public thing for him, not a part of his deepest inner feelings. Only Mama had known his true feelings. And now, maybe, Pearl.

Nobody was watching. He bent over his mother's grave once more and whispered, "I'll always love you, Mama." He felt the lump in his throat and a dampness in his eyes that was not due to the sharp wind. Then he straightened up abruptly and turned away from the grave.

Soon he was heading in long strides down the slope toward the incline station, reassured by the way his lithe body obeyed him. He was still young, vigorous, and a long way from death.

When evening came he hadn't quite shaken off the sadness of the cemetery. He gazed gloomily into the glowing fireplace until Pearl came to cheer him with a soft, fragrant hand on his shoulder. "Thinking of your mama, darling?"

His expression changed, almost too quickly. "No, thinking of the here and now," he said, and wondered for an instant how to make this true. He looked around the room, crowded with heavy furniture. Everything about it seemed dark and old-fashioned

"We can afford a new house in Avondale now," he said. Pearl's eyes lit up.

"I would sooo love to have a solarium," she said. It was the latest innovation in the homes of the wealthy Jews of Avondale. She gave him her sweetest, pleading look.

"Anything for my darling," Jake said.

The next morning, he was already looking at advertisements.

In July 1919 they moved into their new house on Clinton Avenue. It was a corner house that sided on a main street, Reading Road, where everyone could see and admire it. ("It's good business for people to see how well we're doing; wealth makes wealth," Jake said.) There was a huge decorative fountain in the spacious front yard, and the tall windows of the solarium looked out over it.

"The lawn is perfect for Howard and Bernard to play in," said Pearl. "With Lizzie keeping an eye on them, of course."

Hearing herself speak, Pearl was ashamed. *I'll start spending more time with my boys when we are settled in*, she thought. *I won't let them spend so many hours with Lizzie, even though she's a good nursemaid.* But then she had her hands full preparing for the big housewarming party she was planning in August. And afterwards, Jake invited her to join him for a trip to Paris.

The next summer she thought again of spending more time with her sons, and the summer after that, but each time Jake planned another trip abroad. Summer was the only time he could travel; he had his network of suppliers in Europe, and he loved to mix business with pleasure. So she sent the boys to a first-class summer camp instead. "Don't forget to get a haircut before camp," she wrote to Howard from Paris, when she realized she would not even be at home to see her boys off to camp. She felt a twinge of guilt. But Jake's brother Hirsh was sending his children to camp too: Joshua and Hannah and Esther Judith. And it was good for them, wasn't it? Better than spending the summer in the Cincinnati heat.

And so it went, year after year, until it was too late to spend more time with the boys because they were in high school and were busy with whatever it was teenaged boys did with their time: Bernard usually was out playing baseball, and Howard was mostly in his room, reading or writing poetry.

* * *

Photo produced for a magazine ad, February 1921 (Jake on far right).

By 1915, most of Cincinnati's Jews had moved to Walnut Hills or Avondale, leaving behind all the Jewish institutions. Leaving behind such buildings as the beautiful and historic synagogue on Plum Street, the finest in the country, now known as the Isaac M. Wise Temple. Each synagogue now had a building fund, to raise the money for a new building in Avondale. The Adath Israel Synagogue was not a wealthy congregation, but it too moved out to Avondale in 1917. And in modest homes all over the West Side of downtown Cincinnati, less affluent members of the congregation sat around their kitchen tables with pencil and paper, trying to figure out a way to scrimp, save, or borrow the money they needed to move.

An elderly shopkeeper named Lena sat with her husband one sticky summer evening on the West Side. "Do you think we can swing it?" she said. "We can't leave the grandchildren behind downtown." There was silence as they looked at the figures the husband had written down. "Our son-in-law Harry hasn't got much of a head for business. He'll never be able to make the move." They were not ashamed of their son-in-law; Harry Touff was an honest man and a scholar, respected by many people in the Orthodox community. But he depended mostly on his in-laws and his wife's income from her shop to keep afloat, and now they would have to help out once again. They looked at the figures for a while in silence.

Finally Lena spoke. "If we can afford a two-family house in Avondale, you could give Harry a loan." And the husband looked skeptical and said, "Right. A loan."

The elderly couple moved in the summer of 1923, bringing along their daughter, their hapless son-in-law Harry, and the granddaughters. It was a move up the social scale, or a move to be among other Jews—whichever way you wanted to see it. The following September, Harry's daughter Helen, a friendly, brown-eyed girl, was enrolled at Hughes High School. Her new school friends were Jewish girls and boys who lived in the neighborhood.

* * *

On a September day in 1925, Helen received an invitation for a Sunday afternoon signed "Esther Judith Manischewitz." She showed it to her family.

"Well, what do you know?" her mother said. "You move to a different neighborhood, and you change your friends."

"Manischewitz, the rich matzo family, how nice," said her grandmother Lena, who lived downstairs and never missed anything that was going on. "It's not the beautiful house with the fountain, is it? But it must be fancy-schmancy too. You'll have to look at all the furnishings so you can describe them to me later."

Harry took the invitation in his hand and examined it. "That's right . . . This one is the family rabbi, Hirsh. Let's see, it has been how long now?"

He paused, counting the years to himself. "I guess ten years, maybe— since Behr Manischewitz died. May he rest in peace." Harry shook his head. Most people remembered Behr Manischewitz as an prominent personage in the Jewish community. But Harry knew the person behind the public image, the busy man relaxing for a few precious hours over a cup of tea in the little apartment over Harry's wife's shop – maybe the only place where he could just be himself, an older man with plenty of worries that he seldom shared with others.

An older man?

At this point in his thoughts Harry could not help saying, as many a middle-aged man has said before him: "You know, he was still young when he died, but he seemed old to me at the time!"

Helen snatched the invitation and went to her room, embarrassed by all the fuss.

On Sunday, she walked to the home of the Hirsh Manischewitz family on Forest Avenue. Esther Judith welcomed her at the door. She wore a simple dress, and her light hair was in a short, stylish cut. Helen looked into a pair of shy, very blue eyes.

"My name at home is Esther, but my name at school is Judy," she explained self-consciously.

They walked into the sitting room together.

Helen looked around the room so that she would be able to describe it to her grandmother. The furniture was heavy and dark, and in her view altogether uninteresting, compared to the graceful lines of her grandmother's tiny but sweet French living room set. An imposing portrait occupied a prominent spot on the wall. A bearded man looked down from it with such an intense gaze that Helen's eyes were naturally drawn to him.

"My grandfather, who founded the matzo company," Judy explained. There was a poignant mixture of pride and fatigue in her voice. "My uncle Jake had it made from a photograph. But he gave it to my papa to keep."

The weariness in Judy's voice caught Helen's attention. What was it like to be a daughter of the famous family?

The afternoon at Judy's house was meant to be a meeting. Judy had invited girls from several different classes at Hughes High School, where Judy was two years behind Helen, and Walnut

Hirsh and family, 1926 – rear: Joshua, Hirsh, Sara, Hannah;
front: Esther Judith, Natalie, William.

Hills High School, to discuss how to organize their Zionist activities. But the girls from Walnut Hills had sent a note excusing themselves.

"It is no use having a meeting of just the two of us," Judy said. "So we'll just have a social visit."

The two girls went upstairs to Judy's room and sat down on her bed, just inside the door. The window and the better half of the room belonged to Judy's older sister.

"Do you have a lot of friends at the high school?" Judy asked. Her voice was wistful.

Helen had a group of friends at the high school. She boasted shyly about a cute boy named Bubs who sometimes offered to walk her home from school. "He's tall and dark and looks like a

Manischewitz Consanguinity Club picnic, 1926.

movie actor," she told Judy. There was another one, named Sam, "a little too fat but a lot of fun," who had taken her out to a dance. "And he's the one who wants to become an actor, not Bubs," she said.

It was Judy's turn to speak.

"My life is, well, mostly family," she said. "We have a cousins' club. My father and my uncles say that we have to be close to our cousins because some day we will carry on the matzo business together. At least the boys will. We call it the Manischewitz Consanguinity Club."

The club had regular meetings, gave parties, and organized contests for which their parents awarded prizes.

"My cousin Bernard and I usually win the most prizes, because we do the most preparation when there is a contest, and sometimes we prepare together. Then there is my cousin Howard, he is two years older than us and could win more prizes, but he doesn't care to exert himself." She said this in a tone of disapproval. "Unless it's a poetry contest."

Judy had a lot more to say about her family, and much of it was about her cousin Bernard.

William (Bill) in his Sabbath outfit,
Jerusalem, 1928.

Judy and her cousins led a privileged life: piano lessons, expensive sleep-away camps in the summer, horseback riding, drama. Helen thoroughly enjoyed Judy's stories and had a pleasant afternoon in the younger girl's company. She had no thought of jealousy, having somehow been born without the gene that carries that trait.

At last Judy brought the conversation back to the original reason for their meeting.

"It is a shame about the other girls. Sometimes I think they don't believe Palestine is real. I was born there, so believe me, it's real."

Helen was silent. As a little girl, she had collected money for the Jewish National Fund. Once, a German Jewish woman who answered the door had stopped her husband, whose hand was reaching for his wallet, with the admonishment, "You mustn't give her any money. Our Jewish homeland is right here, not in Palestine." Helen had been appalled. But was Palestine real to her?

"I don't remember anything about it." Judy's voice was sad. "We left when I was a baby. My father studied in a yeshiva there. And my second brother is studying there right now."

"My father studied in a yeshiva too, but his was in Lithuania," Helen said. "Is your brother at a yeshiva?"

Judy nodded. "For the whole school year." Again, she sounded almost envious. Helen wondered at this. Weren't yeshivas strict boarding schools where boys wore long black coats? But a photo of the absent brother on Judy's dresser showed a grinning boy in smart-looking white pants and white sun helmet. She wanted to know more, but Judy changed the subject.

"My parents are really strict," Judy said. "Is your father the same?"

Helen was too embarrassed to say that it was her mother and grandmother who dealt out most of the orders at home. But she said something, and Judy replied, and the conversation drifted pleasantly on, until it was time to leave.

"I'll invite you again, when the other girls can come also," Judy promised.

But nothing came of the planned meetings with the girls from the other high school. The next year both girls joined a Zionist youth movement, Young Judaea, but because of the difference in their ages, they were not together.

In 1929 *Der Tag*, the New York Jewish newspaper, announced a contest for two Jewish girls to be elected Queen Esther and her lady-in-waiting. The winners would receive a trip to Palestine.

At sixteen, Judy was used to seeing her older sister Hanna receive most of the praise at home. She nearly fainted with excitement when her family proposed that she enter the contest. "With your big blue eyes—the evil eye shouldn't hear of it—you're sure to win," said her mother. "We'll tell everyone to be sure and vote," offered her brother Joshua. "My girls are all beautiful," said her father, whose role of company rabbi had not made him indifferent to feminine beauty. "When they see your blue eyes, you'll be the queen for sure."

Helen's family were just as confident.

"After you win the first round of selection, God willing, your mother and I will sew something fashionable for you to wear to New York for the final selection," said her grandmother. "Lavender, I think, with your coloring."

But it was blue-eyed Judy Manischewitz who was chosen to go to New York, and who became Queen Esther's lady-in-waiting, and won the trip to Palestine. "This trip to Palestine is the first thing I can say that I have truly accomplished on my own," she wrote on the first page of her trip diary, and sighed with pleasure. Her love for Palestine would last a lifetime.

The contest was the subject of heated discussion in Helen's home. "Our Helen is prettier than either of the winners," protested her grandmother. "I think they bought the votes," said her mother. "The balloting was secret, so you can't prove it," said her sister Roselyn, a serious, rational young woman. "Beauty contests—is this a Jewish thing to do?" said Harry, thumping the table for emphasis.

* * *

About a year later Judy called on Helen again. At seventeen, Judy was the leader of a Young Judaea group of eleven-year-olds. "Would you like to lead a Zionist group?" she asked Helen.

"I can't, because I have to start college in September, at the University of Cincinnati," Helen said.

In September, the boy who sat next to her in her college classroom, and fell in love with her, was Judy's cousin, Howard Manischewitz.

Helen had dated other boys, but she fell in love with Howard at first sight. She loved his wit, his poetic soul, his intelligence—

Helen and Howard at Coney Island.

or maybe it was his debonair charm, or his sparkling blue eyes with dark lashes, or his curly black hair. Whatever she loved in him—and love is, after all, hard to define—it was not the fact that he belonged to a wealthy family.

The burden of a famous name made itself felt even before the engagement. Helen received endless comments from her friends, and even from strangers, on her cleverness in dating the rich Manischewitz boy. By the time the young couple had been going out together for a year, and were both in their second year at the University of Cincinnati, Helen was learning to ignore the comments.

One spring evening, a couple of weeks after Passover 1929, their romance was rudely intruded upon.

Jake Manischewitz summoned his two sons to his home office for an announcement.

"It's time to transfer our manufacturing to the East Coast," Jake told his sons. "So we're moving to New York."

Without waiting for an answer, he went on.

"We'll keep the house in Cincinnati, and we'll live in the Navarro Hotel for a while. I've got my eye on a factory site in Jersey City."

Howard and Bernard were silent. What was the point in replying? Father's word was law. They left his presence as soon as possible, heading out in separate directions into the light spring evening.

Howard spent the rest of the evening on Helen's front porch, where the young lovers sat for hours, holding hands and talking so softly that not even the most curious little sister, or most anxious grandmother, could overhear them.

Bernard spent those same hours at his cousins' house, the Hirsh Manischewitz home on Forest Avenue. There he exploded in loud outrage to the sympathetic ears of his cousin Judy. Then he went outside and played ball with her brother Joshua under the porch light till late in the night.

While his sons let out their frustration—each in his own way—Jake Manischewitz stood calmly before the wide window in the solarium of his home.

His thoughts were on his business.

How smart he'd been to send Meyer and Max to New York years ago. He was so young then—how had he ever thought to do that? It had kept them out of his way, kept them from interfering with running the company.

The two brothers who had stayed in Cincinnati were no problem because they knew their place.

Joseph never caused any trouble—he didn't have the courage for it. Didn't he live in the Belvedere Apartments just to be safe in case of a tornado—even though the last one was nearly twenty years ago?

And Hirsh was no problem. He got enough satisfaction from his role as religious shepherd to the company.

Yes, Jake had foreseen everything.

And now it was time to call in his markers. It was time for the brothers in New York, Meyer and Max, to pay their keep. Com-

Jake in 1932.

panies that limited themselves to just one location eventually stopped growing, and he intended for the matzo company to grow.

There were lots of good models. There was Oscherwitz, who'd come over from Europe on the boat with his father. They had got their start together—two penniless Jews from Europe. The butcher expanded as much as he could in Cincinnati, and then in 1923 he sent his two younger sons to open a sausage factory in Chicago, which was the best place for a sausage business. Just as New York was the best place for a matzo business.

The New York sales office already had plenty to do. There were more Jewish grocers in New York than anywhere else in the world. Plus, New York was a more convenient base than Cincinnati for shipping matzos all over the world—to customers in Europe and Australia and New Zealand.

There was hot competition in New York. He would have to be on the lookout or be overtaken. Horowitz, for instance—a baker from Hungary who'd started a matzo business around the same time as Behr had started in Cincinnati.

Meyer and Max had done well for the company, and even better for themselves personally. Meyer had bought a hotel, the Broadway Central. He did this while drawing a salary from the family business, and he used the name Manischewitz as a guarantee that the hotel's catering was strictly kosher (which it was). No doubt the name had contributed a lot to the success of the hotel's ballrooms for kosher Jewish affairs. But the hotel would come in handy. It would provide cost-free office space and meeting rooms. These were hard times, and plenty of businesses had gone under. It was no time to over-extend himself.

By the time Jake finished reviewing his thoughts, the solarium where he stood was as dark as the yard outside. The oversized potted plants formed spooky shadows on the walls.

A light shone in from the entry hall. It was Pearl, back from an evening out with her sister. She dropped her coat on a chair and walked over to him, bringing with her a whiff of the outdoor air, mixed with her sweet perfume.

"Having good thoughts, darling?" she asked. Her manicured hand reached out to him, brushing his cheek lightly.

"Thinking of New York. And how it will suit you to live there, my love."

In an instant his business worries were far from his mind. He saw himself making love to his wife passionately in a luxurious New York hotel room, after a night out on Broadway. He was eager to be in bed with her now.

He put his arm around her waist, and they wove their way through the room and up the winding staircase.

Long after Jake and Pearl lay peacefully on their silk sheets, tired from lovemaking, their two sons returned home.

Doors opened and closed, and then the house was silent.

* * *

It was an evening of turmoil at Helen's house. After Howard left, Helen tried to slip quietly upstairs to her room. Her mother and grandmother converged upon her.

Meyer, Jake, Joseph, Max, and Hirsh in New York, 1932.

"What about your engagement?" her mother asked. "Did you get some commitment from him?"

Helen took a step back. "Howard will write to me. Good night, Mother, Grandmother," she said, and headed for the stairs.

"It's her own life," said her mother.

"If he's her destiny, he'll come back for her," said her grandmother.

And so Helen's family waited to see what would become of Helen and her romance with the Manischewitz boy.

Meanwhile, the Manischewitz family was consolidating itself in New York. They bought a factory on Bay Street in Jersey City.

Hirsh Manischewitz's family soon prepared to leave for New York. Hirsh Manischewitz was an important man in Cincinnati's Jewish community. He was president of the Orthodox Jewish Orphans Home, and the Welfare Fund for Palestine, and of the Cincinnati branches of many charities and organizations that supported yeshivas in Palestine. In New York, he would be even more active. His Jerusalem-born wife, Sarah, would plunge into charitable activities. Gossips pointed out that Hirsh's oldest daughter, Hannah, was still unmarried—hopefully she would be more likely to find an eligible man in New York.

Judy rejoiced silently over her parents' decision to move. She was in love with her cousin Bernard.

All through 1931, Howard wrote to Helen from New York. "Howard doesn't want to work in the matzo company," Helen told her family. He was planning a more creative career, writing or maybe photography.

His younger brother Bernard, meanwhile, was already at the matzo factory, learning the business from the bottom up. He was being trained by Cousin Max, Jake's old buddy from the days of his courtship of Pearl. Cousin Max was supervisor of the factory now.

On July 19, 1932 Bernard and Judy Manischewitz married in New York. Because they were first cousins, the party was smaller than it would otherwise have been. A marriage of cousins was not exactly forbidden by the Jewish religion, but it wasn't encouraged. The cousins were both just nineteen.

It was this fact that jolted the more philosophical Howard into action. He didn't want a big formal wedding either, so he rushed off to Cincinnati and announced his plans to his parents by telegram: "I want your permission to elope," he wrote, and Jake—amused—consented. Helen and Howard were married in Cincinnati on August 18, 1932, by an Orthodox rabbi, Eliezer Silver, in his study. There was nobody present but the rabbi's wife and another witness or two.

"Which is quite enough, when two young Jewish people have decided to join themselves in wedlock, may God grant them long life together," said Rabbi Silver. The president of the Union of Orthodox Rabbis, he had already served the Manischewitz family on several occasions since his move to Cincinnati a year earlier.

After the ceremony the newlyweds made a brief stop at Helen's house. It wasn't much of a wedding celebration.

"The main thing is the ring on her finger!" said the bride's mother. And that was that.

The next morning Helen and Howard took the train to New York and went to stay at the Navarro Hotel with Jake and Pearl. Helen enrolled at Hunter College in New York, and Howard began to work at photography.

* * *

Pearl's charm was contagious, her laughter was musical. And her romance with her husband was still just as fresh after twenty-two years of marriage as it had been when they were courting. Howard kept a diary filled with observations on his parents. One passage went:

> Father went up the Empire State Building last Thursday, during the big thunderstorm. He said he wanted to learn about electric power.

Another passage read:

> Mother always manages to soothe Father's nerves, when he returns from a hard day at work. He is usually upset about my uncles: "Damn it, they did nothing but play cards all last week while I was in Chicago!" or about my brother: "What does Bernard understand about accounts? He has baseball on his mind, not matzos!" Then Mother pats his cheek and speaks sweetly to him, and all is well.

* * *

The company's fortunes were shaky during the years of the Great Depression. But it was like winning a chess game to Jake Manischewitz, and his optimism was contagious.

Howard was skeptical. "Let's hope that the Passover season will pull Dad out of his financial troubles," he wrote in his diary. "The next three months will disclose our fate."

There was a flood in Cincinnati in March, which did not help matters. The factory was unharmed, but a flood always meant delivery problems. The railroad tracks used by the factory were on low ground near the Mill Creek, which often flooded along with the Ohio River.

In June 1933, Jake and Pearl and Howard and Helen attended the World's Fair in Chicago. Bernard stayed behind in New York with Judy, pleased to be left in charge of the factory.

Helen sent a postcard from the Fair to her family in Cincinnati. "We're staying in a nice modern hotel," she wrote. "Jake and Pearl are staying at the Congress Hotel, which is old and very elegant. We're all having a wonderful time."

But when they returned to New York, Pearl was deathly ill. Howard wrote in his diary:

> Mother is desperately ill, and seems to get weaker daily. Doctor F has not the slightest idea what her sickness is. One moment he tells us she is nearly well, and the next he tells us that if she is not better by the first of August, he will operate. We wait and hope for her recovery.

The doctor decided to operate. Pearl died of the operation on August 8, 1933, just six days after her forty-fifth birthday.

Jake was devastated. He cut himself off from the reality of her death, refusing to touch anything of Pearl's, refusing even to enter the room they had shared. It was Howard who saved his mother's personal possessions and her precious box of correspondence from destruction. And it was Howard who cried over her last letter:

Dearest Jack,

You may not realize it, but I can honestly assure you that in the midst of my sickness my mind is continually on you and was always on you, but of course I never let you see it. You looked more cheerful today and it has made me happier. I am not going to write you a lot of "slush" because I am over that school girl period, but I will tell you this, that you have in my estimation saved my life so far, with your wonderful devotion and love, and I do love you more than ever, if that were possible. You have been very good and patient with me and I want you to know that I have not been ungrateful, even if I have seemed so at times. Take care of yourself darling. Lots of love and kisses from your sweetheart,
Pearl

The facts of Pearl's death were only known months later. "Chicago Epidemic Was Kept Secret," the headlines announced. There had been an epidemic of amoebic dysentery at the Chicago World's Fair, at the height of the summer season. The city authorities withheld the information about the epidemic, so as not to ruin the financial success of the fair. Some victims were suing, and the Congress Hotel was mentioned. Pearl's doctor had treated her without this information, not guessing her real ailment. It was an unnecessary death.

* * *

In September, Jake told Helen and Judy to divide up Pearl's personal possessions between them. He still could not bear the sight of anything that had belonged to her.

Then the family dispersed. Helen and Howard at last moved into an apartment of their own.

Bernard and Judy moved back to Cincinnati, where Bernard was put in charge of the Cincinnati factory, having learned enough a lot about factory work from his hands-on apprenticeship in New Jersey under Cousin Max's tutelage.

Bernard was already planning to outshine his older brother and all of his cousins in the company. He sometimes tried mouthing the words "Bernard Manischewitz, president of the B. Manischewitz Company" in front of his mirror. But he knew that he looked very, very young at twenty. Too young, despite the mustache he had grown. He wouldn't tell anyone about his plan, not yet. They would realize it soon enough.

Howard had not intended to work in the matzo company at all. But between his father's domineering personality— "We need all hands on deck now"—and the harsh reality of the Depression, he changed his plans. He decided to wait till the end of the year and start in January 1934. One by one, his cousins began to work in the company too—the boys from the Cousins' Club. It had been Jake's idea from the start for them all to work together under him.

Jake plunged back into his work, but it wasn't enough to quell his despair, and he could not bear to be alone. His friends and acquaintances knew this.

Bernard with moustache, 1932.

"Jack lives too fast to spend much time on grieving," they said. And so one friend gave the hint to another, and before a month had gone by one of them—his dentist—introduced him to an attractive blond widow.

He remarried before the end of the year, on November 15, 1933. He took his new wife, Ila, to Europe on a honeymoon, which he combined with business in France, England, and Poland.

* * *

Recovering from the shock of the Depression wasn't easy, even for the Manischewitz Company.

The Passover season was a breath of oxygen for the company's finances. Even so, around June 1934, its finances were at their lowest. Jake had rented an elegant apartment in the Essex House to live in with his new wife, and almost immediately had to sub-lease it, moving to a place that cost only half as much. Next, he had to sell his beautiful house in Cincinnati, with the fountain, for the paltry price of eight thousand dollars. He tried to do this discreetly, but Cincinnati's Jews all heard about it.

Hirsh, too, left his nine-room apartment and moved to a smaller one. Hirsh's oldest daughter, Hannah, was married in June in New York. In spite of everything, the family splurged on a big wedding party with five hundred guests. Of course, the party was held at her uncle's hotel, the Broadway Central, which helped to limit costs. Hirsh, too, had to sell his Cincinnati house. This was another transaction that could hardly be done discreetly. A Jewish fraternity of college boys bought the house. The boys had a great time kidding around over their discovery in the base-ment: a ritual bath, or *mikvah*. Hirsh had installed it long ago for his Palestine-born wife Sarah so that she would not need to use a communal one.

By September of the same year, the company's finances had somehow greatly improved. "The stock may even pay dividends in two years," Howard noted in his diary.

Four years later, Howard admitted that his pessimism had been ill-placed.

"This year, 1938, we celebrate the fiftieth anniversary of the B. Manischewitz Company," he wrote in his diary. "The matzo business continues to prosper. The fiscal year will not be as good as last year but will show a substantial profit. Sufficient for a dividend in May. Stock is quoted at 10 ½ bid, 15 asked. Not bad."

* * *

Meanwhile, the clouds of war and anti-Semitism gathered over Europe.

"We're lucky to have no family left in Europe," said Helen's grandmother one Sunday. Many people in Cincinnati did have family in Europe, and they were facing the silence that meant the worst, though nobody knew this yet.

"But Helen, what about the Manischewitz family? Do they have anyone still left in Europe?"

Helen didn't know. She promised to ask her father-in-law when next she saw him.

* * *

Summer, the slow season in the matzo business, was the only time Jake relaxed. The family often gathered at the Manischewitz summer home in New Jersey, a pleasant two-story house with white pillars in front that Jake called Mannhaven. The house had an enormous green lawn, a big shady pavilion, a massive stone outdoor grill, and many big wooden deck chairs scattered about the lawn. The Atlantic Ocean was out of sight, but its presence was felt in a hint of saltiness in the gentle breeze that wafted across the lawn.

It was a warm day in June 1940. When Helen arrived that day at Mannhaven, dressed in a simple shirtwaist dress, there were a number of guests and family members present. A manservant led her directly out to the lawn, where Jake was sitting in a comfortable deck chair, caressing his dog.

Helen was afraid of dogs, so she gave the handsome, dark brown dachshund a wary look.

"Helen, meet Bosco, my best friend," said Jake, by way of a greeting. Someone brought Helen a chair.

"Oh, is his name Bosco?" she asked politely. She sat down carefully, as far as possible from the dog.

One of Jake's brothers, who was standing nearby with a plate, explained the name to her.

"Like the chocolate syrup—it's a brand name."

Helen hadn't heard of it.

"The New York Jews all drink it because it is certified kosher," Jake told her, warming to the subject. "They want kosher all year round."

Several guests came closer to listen.

"Kosher food has come up in the world, I can tell you," Jake continued.

"Ten years ago, the doomsday folks all told me, 'Jews are getting too modern to care about kosher food.' So I said, 'Business will pick up again, just you wait and see.' "

He waited for his listeners to acknowledge how right he had been.

They all nodded. The slump in the matzo business had only been temporary. But perhaps the passing of the Depression had also played a role in its recovery.

"Today kosher food is more popular than ever," Jake went on. "Even the Reformed Jews are changing their tune. 'Kosher means clean,' one of them said to me last week. He thought he had to apologize to me, why is he buying kosher food."

"It's because of the war in Europe," said the uncle, waving his fork for emphasis. "In bad times, Jews remember who they are, they go to the synagogue more often, they go back to their roots."

This caused a lull in the conversation. Everyone was worried about the war in Europe.

Helen decided that this was the right time for her question. "Father, is there anyone of the family still living in Europe?" She spoke hesitantly. Lately, she had noticed, her father-in-law was easily angered. Jake had changed since the death of his beloved Pearl. His life was filled with work and entertainment and his new love, but a woman could see that he was not happy.

He frowned at her question, and shook his head impatiently.

"The only person I have in Europe is my matzo jobber in Vienna. I set him up in thirty-two and brought him over here to learn about the business."

He paused. "I guess I can forget about selling matzos in Europe now, eh?"

*　*　*

On that same June day, the Red Army entered Telz. A shabbily dressed middle-aged man named Jacob watched the Russian soldiers going to and from the yeshiva building, trying to calculate the best course of action for himself and his wife and children.

He was a few years older than his American cousin Jake Manischewitz, who had entirely forgotten about his existence. Jacob had written to the family in America several times in recent years. But Hirsh, who handled all the European correspondence, had not mentioned the letters to Jake.

Jacob had a good head of black hair which made him look younger and healthier than he really was. He was a lot older than most of the soldiers he saw in the doorway. Where were the yeshiva students now that the Red Army had commandeered their building? Scattered in five makeshift study halls, still at their books. His own son, Yitzhak, had quit years ago, to help his mother in the cafe. Rumor had it that two of the rabbis were planning to leave in August to search for a new location for the yeshiva in America. They would do better to take their wives and children with them and never come back, Jacob thought.

Swallowing his shock at the desecration of the building, he went inside and asked to talk with the commanding officer.

When he returned home he spoke solemnly to his wife Chaya and his son Yitzhak. His small daughters listened fearfully.

"I've enlisted in the Lithuanian Division of the Red Army," he said. "It's the best hope for the family. The two of you together don't need my help to run the cafe. My soldier's pay, or my pension if I should die, will be better than nothing."

The next day he was gone.

* * *

The following year, in June 1941, Bernard moved his family back to New York, so that he could participate more directly in managing the company. He was being groomed for his future role as president of the company. Things were going well for Bernard. Only one thing was not going as he had planned, and this was completely out of his hands: he badly wanted an heir to the company, but Judy had given birth only to daughters.

* * *

That same month, the Germans occupied Telz. The Russian army hastily retreated eastward. A few weeks would pass before the Jews of Telz were rounded up. The police roughed up some young Jewish men in the street, and arrested some of them. For the rest, it was a matter of days or weeks. Time enough for Jacob's son, Yitzhak, to decide what to do. He hastily put some food and a change of clothing in a bag and bade his mother farewell. "I love you, Mother," he said. "But I am not going to wait for them to get me." The boy embraced his mother and went to the woods to join the partisans.

On the twentieth of Tammuz, June 27, 1941, all the Jewish men of Telz, including the remaining yeshiva students, were forcibly assembled by the lake on the edge of town and then taken to the woods,

Last photo of Jake, Mannhaven, 1941.

to be shot in the following days by the Nazi murderers and their
Lithuanian accomplices.

Yitzhak was with the partisans now. So he did not see how his
mother and little sisters, together with all of the Jewish mothers and
children and old women of Telz, huddled fearfully for weeks in a another camp, until they too were taken to the edge of a mass grave and
shot.

* * *

In July, Jake again invited family and friends to his summer residence in New Jersey.

He sat in his lawn chair, played with his dog Bosco, and chatted and joked with his wife and their friends. "Have a Tam Tam
cracker," he said, holding out a plate to each of them in turn.

"What is it, Jake?"

"Nothing but a brilliant invention," Jake said. "You have before you the very first product of the Manischewitz Company that has nothing to do with Passover."

His voice was full of pride. The new crackers were selling well. And he was sure that many, many other products would follow.

* * *

Jake's brother Meyer pretended to concentrate on his plate of potato salad as if Jake's boasting did not bother him. Well, his brother could forget about being the only one with brilliant ideas.

Meyer allowed himself a crafty smile. This was one time he had been just as clever as his brother. He had come up with the idea of other projects first, and he had granted use of his name to a noodle manufacturer in New York. Jake had not even found out about it until the noodles were already appearing on the grocery shelves. Then he had to grin and bear it. Meyer had put into the contract an agreement that the license would be transferred to the Manischewitz Company after his death. What did it matter? He had no children. Meanwhile he was raking in the money with no exertion of his own—unlike his brother Jake, who was putting in fourteen-hour days.

Meyer had given the idea to brother Max, who looked docile enough today, innocently munching on the Tam Tam crackers.

But in fact Max had taken the hint and was already looking about for a company to license a new product to. And his idea would turn out to be the best of all.

* * *

Neither Max nor Meyer would live to enjoy their successes for very long. Both brothers died by 1949.

* * *

Tam Tam crackers, the first non-Passover product.

With Bernard taking on more responsibility in New York, Howard was sent to manage the Cincinnati factory, to the great joy of Helen's family.

"Howard doesn't have his father's business sense," said Helen's grandmother, shaking her head anxiously.

Helen's mother nodded. "Right, he's like my Harry—better with books than with practical things."

"But on the other hand, Cincinnati is the backwaters now," observed the grandmother, whose experience as a shopkeeper had taught her a lot about business. "The factory back east is much more important. He'll be okay."

"Howard says he has an old-timer looking out for him," Helen said. "Sam Sloane, the office manager, who worked for Behr Manischewitz in the old days."

"We shouldn't be worried about small things anyway. These are such anxious times for all Jews," said the grandmother.

They were all fearful about the future. What would it mean if Germany won the war? Would anti-Semitic laws eventually be enacted everywhere, even in America?

* * *

March 1942 was an anxious time. Howard was in charge of the matzo factory. The pre-Passover baking was in full swing, and Helen was in the ninth month of a difficult pregnancy.

On Sunday, the twenty-second of March, Helen shared her worries with her mother and grandmother.

"You know what my girlfriends have been saying to me?" she said to them over tea and cookies. "They have been saying, 'How can you want to have a baby, a Jewish baby, in these awful times?'"

"If Jews didn't have babies in awful times, where would we be now?" her mother asked.

A silence followed.

* * *

In the infirmary of the Lithuanian Division in distant Gorky, now known as Nizhny Novgorod, Jacob's body shook with dysentery. It was mid-March 1942 and the division had not yet seen battle. Jacob and many of the other men would die of disease before its first action. On Saturday some new recruits arrived, and one of them came to the infirmary. "Have you any word of the Jews in Telz?" Jacob called out to the newcomer. "Dead, all dead," said the man. "Some may have escaped to the ghetto of Kovno," said a voice from a corner, "and maybe a few are in the woods with the partisans." Jacob died on Sunday, hoping that his son might still be alive. But the boy was already buried under the Lithuanian earth and snow.

* * *

Even though it was Sunday, Jake Manischewitz was hard at work in the factory in Jersey City.

He had been working his hardest for the last three weeks, and sleeping little, as he did every year in March, even though he had been having some symptoms of his weakening heart during the preceding months.

His brothers Meyer and Max took frequent breaks, for the work was too intense for their taste. Even at this crucial time of year, they could sometimes be found in the offices, closeted in one of the smaller rooms.

"Damn it, don't you think I know you've been playing casino back there!"

Max shrugged. "We're here now, right?" He reached nonchalantly for his apron.

On Tuesday afternoon, the twenty-fourth of March, in New York, Jake suddenly stood still. After a whole morning spent leaning over the hot machinery, his face was red with heat and excitement. He wiped his forehead.

"That's all for me, boys," he said to his brothers.

He took off his apron, placing it carefully on a hook, as if he were going home.

But he continued to stand there, looking at the oven, as if thinking of some improvement.

It took a couple of hours for his brothers to realize that something was wrong.

At five o'clock, brother Max took his arm and pulled him away from the room. "I'm driving you home," he said, and became frightened when he saw how passively his brother allowed himself to be steered toward the car.

"I'm tired as a dog," Jake said, in an odd voice. But back at the apartment he revived, and until about eleven he was in splendid spirits and jolly.

"I'm feeling ill again," he told his wife at eleven, and she called the doctor, who came immediately.

He died around midnight.

At four in the morning, all the arrangements were made for the funeral, to be held at three in the afternoon on Thursday.

Jake was fifty-four. He had headed the company since his father's death in 1914. Despite the short notice, over a thousand people attended his funeral in New York. The whole family was present except for Howard, because Cincinnati was too far for him to have arrived on time.

* * *

Howard closed the factory in Cincinnati on the day of the funeral, a little awed at taking such a responsibility. It was the first time the factory had been closed during a Passover baking season in over half a century. Sam Sloane patted him on the back, and assured him that he was doing the right thing.

He was shaken by his father's death and surprised at the depth of his own feelings. He had resented his father's domineering ways, his overpowering personality. And now he discovered how much he loved him. Was his brother Bernard going through the same confused emotions of love and loss?

Helen's family were Howard's safe haven in the four difficult days that followed.

On the fifth day, Helen gave birth to a baby boy. She was groggy from the anesthesia when Howard was admitted to her room at the Jewish Hospital.

"Have you seen our son?" she asked, her voice heavy with anesthesia.

"Just a glimpse," Howard replied, taking her hand. "We'll have to name him for Dad," he added, though he couldn't have explained why.

Would his baby head the Manischewitz Company one day? Was that what the name meant? The tiny boy at the nursery looked so delicate with his wispy brown hair, more like a future poet than a future business mogul. Did Howard even want such a future for his infant son? Or did he only want his brother Bernard—who had no sons—to think so? And where were these thoughts coming from?

Meanwhile, Helen pondered the old-fashioned name. In the 1940s in Cincinnati, Jewish boys were mostly given modern names: Jeffrey, Stanley.

"Jacob?" she asked hesitantly.

"No, Jack," said Howard.

"Oh, yes. The name your father wanted for himself. He was always asking people to call him Jack," said Helen. "But without much success," she added after a moment's thought.

Howard did not reply. The notion of his father as a human being, a man who had his successes, plenty of them, but also some frustrations and maybe a failure or two, was something the son was not ready to deal with.

He had believed his dad was invincible, and now, was Dad really gone?

Helen saw only her husband's grief, not his inner questions. "Jack," she repeated softly. "Jack Manischewitz. A fine name for a baby boy." Then she had another thought.

"You'll have to tell everyone at the Seder tonight that we've chosen a name for the baby."

"The Seder?" said Howard dully. With the mourning and the birth—he had actually forgotten that tonight was the first night of Passover.

Helen smiled. "Another year, another Seder. And next year your son will be at the table, and you will tell him the Passover story."

"While he gurgles the Four Questions," said Howard. And smiled at his own joke, feeling better already.

Because life goes on—a death, a birth, and a holiday, tears and rejoicing, one event following the other in quick succession.

Just as it has always done.

Chapter 8

Afikoman

Afikoman: a slice of matzo which must be eaten at the
end of the meal on the Seder night of Passover.
— *Talmudic Encyclopedia*

The days of mourning are normally seven in Jewish tradition, but
the mourning for Jake Manischewitz was over almost as soon it
started. For the tradition also decrees that it is forbidden to
mourn on the Passover holiday.

Sadness is not so easily regulated—but fortunately, neither is
rejoicing. At the Cincinnati home of Howard and Helen Manischewitz, the sentiments were mixed. On the eighth day, with the
circumcision of baby Jack, joy clearly took the upper hand.

"Just look at my son's big blue eyes." Howard was usually the
cynic of the family, but on this day he was elated as seldom before in his life. He had been taking photos all afternoon. Now he
set down the bulky camera and disconnected the giant screen-
covered spotlights, relics of his six-month alternative career as a
professional photographer.

"Would you believe what you see before you?" he said, to anyone who might be listening. "Another generation of men to carry
on the Manischewitz dynasty!"

Helen looked down lovingly at the newly circumcised baby in
her arms. In fact she had been admiring the baby almost non-
stop for eight days now: her little miracle; her long-awaited son
after several miscarriages and a precarious pregnancy.

"Now Howard," she said in a teasing voice, "I thought you didn't want our son to ever go into the matzo business? Too constraining, too whatever, the usual complaints."

Howard shrugged.

"Father's four brothers are still going strong," he decreed. We won't even need to *think* about the future of the Manischewitz Company for decades."

Helen nodded. "So all you boys from the Cousins' Club will have easy sailing." Most of the cousins were in New York. Howard did seem to have a quiet niche, managing the Cincinnati factory. It was not where the action was—but so what? Howard was not competing with anybody. He was a poet at heart, and nurtured the hope of writing a great novel in his free time.

Howard sat down. Easy sailing was exactly what he wanted.

"Long enough for little Jackie and a dozen other future Manischewitz boys to take their time growing up," he predicted.

He did not say whether he intended to father the whole tribe of boys himself.

But fate has a way of ignoring all our prognostics, cynical or otherwise.

For the first few months things went in the direction that Howard (and his brother and cousins) expected. In June, at the meeting of the board of directors, Meyer Manischewitz, eldest of the brothers, was elected president of the company. At the same time a one dollar per share dividend was declared on the common stock for the semester. Eventually the presidency would rotate to Joseph.

"All's well with the company, thank God," said Hirsh to his wife Sarah after that first board meeting. "If only we could have the same reassurance about the fate of our people in Europe." Because of his religious background, Hirsh felt very affected—probably more than his brothers—by the fate of Jews outside the Golden Land of America. Sarah immediately added, "With God's help." After a hard childhood in Jerusalem, she knew very well how precarious the life of Jews could be, anywhere but in America.

In fact, despite the war in Europe, 1942 was the best year since 1937 for the company in terms of sales and profit. The war (which, of course, halted sales of matzos in Europe) had brought many American Jews, grateful for their own safety, back to the traditional family table. "Profits are up," Howard noted in his diary, "and stock is inactive. Only 315 holders and tightly held. Last sale was at 8 ½."

But on October 9 of the following year Hirsh Manischewitz—youngest of the brothers, rabbi, and vice president of the company—was stricken by heart failure while attending services at Congregation Ohab Zedek. It was shortly after two on the afternoon of Yom Kippur, in the midst of the solemn Unesanneh Tokef prayer, which includes the phrase "who shall live, and who shall die." One moment the holy words of the prayer were in his mouth, the next moment he stuttered and coughed. His startled neighbors on each side grasped his arms and held him upright, too frightened to think of any other action. Within moments his spirit left him, and his lifeless body sank back into the seat as they cautiously, tremblingly released their hold. Almost before the prayer ended, the officiating rabbi hastened to their side. He explained to the frightened men as gently as possible that under Jewish law, Hirsh's body could not be touched until the blowing of the shofar at the conclusion of the services for the day. It was a day that seemed to last for an eternity as the awe-struck congregation, a dead man seated among them, prayed for God to turn aside His harsh judgment of the living.

When dusk came and the awesome blowing of the shofar finally broke the tension, a small group hastened to bring Hirsh's body to a side room, where Rabbi Dr. Jacob Hoffman, deeply moved, arranged for it to remain until the funeral there the following day, Sunday, at two. (This was a very unusual honor; Jewish funerals are almost never held in the synagogue.) Thousands of people crowded Ohab Zedek for the funeral, including hundreds of rabbis and other leaders of Jewish life. Other hundreds who could not gain admittance lined the streets until the funeral procession made its way to the Riverside Cemetery in New Jersey. At the time of his death Hirsh was president of the Orthodox Jewish Orphan Home and active in many national and international philanthropic organizations, including charities for the Jews in Palestine.

At about this time the directorship passed to Joseph.

The next brother to die was Meyer, on July 16, 1944. He had continued to run the 500-room Broadway Central Hotel until his death. (His widow would sell the hotel a year later and move to California.) The hotel had grown to be something of a landmark in New York. The family had used it for many purposes over the years, ever since Jake's decision to move the main focus of the matzo company to New York. It was the only hotel in New York with facilities to cater kosher banquets for as many as 3,000 guests at one sitting. It was also, perhaps, the only kosher hotel to house a night club. Meyer had made that addition in 1940 because, as he told journalists tongue-in-cheek, the hotel "needs a spot of color." "Fun-loving and festive himself," said the journalist, describing Meyer, "Mr. Manischewitz good-naturedly supposes that his newest enterprise will be accepted in that spirit."

Meyer was sixty-one when he died.

The noodle company that Meyer had created, with little effort beyond selling his name to a manufacturer, reverted to the Manischewitz Company upon his death.

At last the war in Europe ended. Jewish families all across America waited in hope and fear as the news of their worst nightmares was revealed. Tens of thousands of survivors arrived and told their stories of horror. It was necessary to have a family's address in America in order to obtain a visa and leave the displaced persons camps in Europe. At least one resourceful woman who had survived the war under dramatic conditions waited for long months in a DP camp, unable to learn the address of her rela-

tives in Ohio. Then, on the first Passover of freedom, Manischewitz matzos were distributed in the camp. She wrote to the factory address in Cincinnati that she found on the box. An
employee of the company located her family for her.

But among all the letters that crossed the ocean, no letter ever
arrived from the relatives of Behr Manischewitz in Lithuania.

Every one of them had perished.

The postwar years.

The year 1947 was perhaps the luckiest year of all for the Manischewitz family, though nobody realized it at the time. For Max,
at age fifty-seven, decided it was high time to follow Meyer's example of seeking out a way to add to his income by arranging for
a new product that could be produced without any hard work
on his own part. Max's scheme was even better than his brother's,
for he chose the one product (apart from matzo) most laden with
tradition and warm feelings and love in the hearts of Jews everywhere, the one product most certain to grace everyone's Sabbath
and holiday table: kosher wine.

He located a company, Monarch Wine, that agreed to follow
the very stringent rules governing the production of kosher wine,
from the grape to the bottle, and under totally reliable supervision. Max explained everything to them in detail, feeling very
proud that he still remembered it so well from his yeshiva days so
long ago in Jerusalem. Then he signed a license allowing them to
put the Manischewitz name on the bottles. Once the arrangements were in place, and the strict supervision was guaranteed,
Max didn't have to lift a finger; he simply received a royalty of 15
cents on every bottle sold. Just as his brother had done with the
noodle company, Max signed a contract under which the royal-
ties from sales of wine reverted to the Manischewitz Company
after his death. After all, like Meyer, he had no children. The contract was to run until 2040, and Max expected to gain some forty
thousand dollars a year for himself right from the start, plus profit
as a major stockholder in the company.

It looked like a comfortable retirement was in the stars for Max. But not even a year went by before he was dead, stricken by a heart attack at the Beverly-Wilshire Hotel in Los Angeles.

Of the five brothers, Joseph alone remained. He was president of the company now. His son D. Beryl was promptly given the position of vice president of the New Jersey factory. His younger son, deemed unsuited to working under pressure, was sent off to Canada on some vague business assignment. Howard was still manager of the Cincinnati factory. And Bernard? Whatever title he was given, Bernard had pretty much taken over the running of the company, just as he had dreamed of doing from age nineteen, the year he grew the little mustache and started learning the ropes from his father's old buddy and distant cousin Max, the foreman.

Meanwhile, Joseph's health was faltering, and he was scared. No, make that terrified. His four brothers were already dead of heart failure. Joseph had had a first heart attack twenty years earlier, and he was having chest pains more and more frequently. He was short of breath, though his doctor said this was only normal for a heavy smoker, and not related to his heart. His brothers had also been heavy smokers, and smoking had never stopped Jake from putting in a full day's work. Joseph left Bernard and the cousins in charge of the company, even though it was the busiest time of the year, and headed for Florida, hoping that somehow the sun and relaxation would stave off the inevitable.

It was no use. He died of a heart ailment on March 28, 1949, in Miami Beach.

Once again the factory (both factories) closed for a funeral right in the midst of Passover baking. "And so the last of Dad's brothers is gone, all in the space of just seven years," Howard wrote in his diary. "What will become of us now?"

Yet in reality, nothing much changed. For with Joseph ill in Florida for many weeks before Passover, the future setup of the New York operation was already in place, and only needed to be formalized. Bernard became president, D. Beryl became chairman, and Hirsh's second son, William, was treasurer. Hirsh's older son, Joshua, who did not seem to be cut out for management, was given a less prominent position. And Howard continued as manager of the Cincinnati plant.

The next decade was family time for the members of the newly responsible younger generation. In Cincinnati, little Jack soon had a baby sister, Laura. In New York, Bernard and Judy were raising their two small daughters, Elaine and Rubye. (Much later they would have a third daughter.) Howard and Bernard's cousin D. Beryl (Joseph's son) had a son, David, and a daughter; Beryl's younger son, Robert, was not destined to have children. Hirsh's first son, Joshua, had just one son, Hirsh, but the boy's health was fragile. Hirsh's second son, William Beryl (Bill), had a sickly son who died at age ten, and his first marriage ended in divorce.

Bernard's family, 1953 –
left to right: Rubye/Rivka, Elaine, Judy, Bernard.

Howard's family, 1959 – left to right: Helen, Jack, Laura, Howard.

William (Bill)'s family in Teaneck, NJ –
left to right: Ofra, Bill, Esther, Liora, Sharon.

Where were the masses of Manischewitz sons foreseen by Howard when Jack was born? There were plenty of daughters. But, as in the preceding generation, daughters were considered of no relevance to the company. Only a son or grandson with the family name would be considered an heir.

In 1951 Bill married again and celebrated his wedding in Bernard's plush apartment on Central Park West. His bride was from Jerusalem, from an Orthodox family whose ties with the Manischewitz family went back a long way: Hirsh had made the connection during his own yeshiva studies. From this marriage came more daughters: Liora, Ofra, Sharon. All bright, lovely girls—and irrelevant to the future of the Manischewitz Company.

And so, with each passing year, the continuation of the family matzo business into the next generation became less likely. There were broader factors at work too. Jewish families in the fifties were raising their sons to be intellectuals, doctors and lawyers, not to run family businesses. Howard and Helen were like so many other Jewish parents: when their son took an early interest in biology, they encouraged him to aim for long years of university study. Beryl's son David was interested in the world of business, but he also undertook long years of study, becoming so highly skilled that only Wall Street was a suitable place of employment for him. His participation in the family business would be as a consultant and, eventually, a board member: not as a roll-up-your-sleeves factory trainee to fill Bernard's shoes.

So Bernard settled in for the long term: there would be no heirs to take over from him. Would things have gone differently if he had actively encouraged his nephew, or his cousin's son, or even one of his own daughters or their husbands, to enter the business? Nobody can say. And nobody—least of all the daughters—even asked such questions until many years had passed.

Bernard had already proved his competence by making some smart moves. In 1954 the company purchased a processing plant in Vineland, New Jersey, for the manufacture of borscht, chicken soup, and gefilte fish.

The children of the next generation were spread out geographically, between Cincinnati and the Greater New York area. There was no Cousins' Club to bring them together, and contact was only on special occasions. When Jack reached thirteen, his Bar Mitzvah was held in Bernard's spacious apartment on Central Park West. He and his sister walked from room to room, discovering the oddity of their cousins' home, which lacked a grassy backyard but contained more rooms than their Cincinnati house.

In 1958 the factory in Cincinnati was closed. This was a minor detail to most of the family, already settled in the New York area. For Howard and his family, it was a big move from Cincinnati, where every Jewish family knew their parents and grandparents. Teenaged Jack and Laura faced new schools in New Jersey—and new classmates teasing them by singing the "Man Oh Manischewitz" advertising jingle which had preceded their arrival. Helen left the tightly knit circle of her own family in Cincinnati. Howard became advertising manager, playing second fiddle (not surprisingly) to his brother and cousins, who had strengthened their positions in the company over decades in the Jersey City factory.

Behr's love for the Holy Land had left its impact on the family and on the company, even though the orange groves he had purchased in his firm belief in a Jewish state had long since been confiscated. Almost as soon as the infant State of Israel was proclaimed in 1948, Bernard and a member of his managerial staff, Haim Pomeranz, made a trip to Israel to see about establishing a matzo factory there. A second trip with his wife in 1950 yielded no results, but led to the formation of new links in the young State of Israel. In 1956 Bernard's eldest daughter, Elaine, sailed for Israel and met her husband there, a young Yemenite immigrant.

And so, on the eve of the 1960s, the next foray into Israel fit right into context. With great enthusiasm, Bill moved to Israel for a couple of years with his wife, Esther, and their three growing daughters, hoping to establish both a branch of the company and his own family's future there. But it did not work out as he hoped. As before, there did not seem to be the right conditions for establishing a factory in Israel. Or maybe it was just the wrong time, due to conditions back at home. Discouraged, Bill returned to New Jersey and to his former position in the company.

"Passover 1961 was a bad time," Judy wrote in a notebook that she labeled "Significant Dates in My Life." It was the year of one of the very few initiatives that did not work out: a plan for the company to do its own distribution. Bernard and Judy spent Passover in Israel that year. It was an error; a lot of money was lost over the Passover season. The next year, the company returned to the old distribution system, and Bernard and Judy gave up their apartment on Central Park West to cut expenses.

This setback definitely wasn't something Bernard intended to talk about when Howard invited the entire family, in the summer of 1961, to his house in West Orange for a fiftieth birthday celebration (Howard's birthday was in March, but in the Manischewitz family, summer was a much better time for a party).

It was a rare occasion for a family get-together. New Jersey was not like Cincinnati, where all the Jews had lived in a couple of compact neighborhoods. The metropolitan area radiated out from Jersey City, north to Teaneck, where Bill's family lived, and west all the way to White Meadow Lake, where Bernard already owned the weekend getaway that was soon to be his permanent home.

Somewhere between the main course and the dessert, Laura asked her father a question that had been on her mind. She was sixteen, a good time for questioning one's elders.

"So we know how great the last generation was," she said, "because you're always talking about them. But what has your generation accomplished for the matzo business?"

Howard had a ready answer. "Kept it from going under," he said promptly. "You know how many hundreds of businesses didn't last so long?"

Bernard and Judy at cousins' party, 1961.

"Okay, so how did you do it?" She didn't have to wait for an answer.

"Good advertising, of course," said Howard, who was the advertising manager. "Look at the *Food Store Review*, for instance. Goes to every single mom-and-pop Jewish grocery in the country." Howard was the editor of the magazine, which had been going since 1941.

Bill leaned over from the next table to put in a word. "I would say something very different, Laura." Bill was active in the Orthodox Jewish community. "I would say it is definitely because of the way we positioned the company in the Jewish community, in Jewish affairs, with the religious Jews. Manischewitz is a name that Jewish people can trust."

Beryl listened and said nothing, keeping his own counsel, as he often did.

Joshua was busy at another table, tasting the food and abundantly praising Helen for her cooking—though in fact the strictly kosher meal had been catered.

Bernard waited to have the last word, as he often did.

"New products," he said. "Getting new products on the market. Without growth, you die." At that, he turned his attention back to the buffet.

The discussion of business was over for the day.

The next generation may not have had Behr's or Jake's stamina when it came to rolling up their sleeves in front of a hot oven. But they were all longer-lived than their fathers' generation. The women of the family (who would, not surprisingly, outlive the men) never played a role in the company. But—if Bill was right about the importance of community relations—the women did matter after all. In their personal capacity, many of the women of the family were active in Jewish affairs and especially in activities for Israel. Judy chaired a weekend Israel festival in 1968. In 1971 she received the Eleanor Roosevelt Humanities Award from the Franklin and Eleanor Roosevelt Institute for service to humanity and devoted support to Israel. Helen became active in her local Hadassah chapter; she had served as president of the Cincinnati chapter before moving east. Hirsh's widow, Sarah, was active in many charitable activities within the Orthodox community, such as an organization collecting funds for wedding gowns to be provided to orphan brides in Jerusalem. She continued her charitable works well into her nineties.

Meanwhile, the men of the family—with Bernard as president, his brother and cousins in various other positions—continued to run the company until 1972, when they turned its operational reins over to a team of professional managers. However, majority ownership of the company remained with the Manischewitz family.

In 1981, through a license agreement, the company began manufacturing and distributing Goodman's matzo and matzo products. One less competitor.

In what seemed to have become a sad family tradition, Howard died of a heart attack just before Passover. The year was 1984, and he was seventy-three—not as old as his wife and son and daughter would have wished him to become, but older than any of the men in the previous generation. The small family that gathered for the funeral was already far-flung: Jack lived with his wife in Maryland, and Laura was living with her family in Switzerland. Nobody had ever expected a branch of the family to return to live in Europe, but there they are: Laura and her husband Joseph (Yossi) and two daughters, settled more or less permanently in Switzerland. It wasn't something they had planned: like Bill and his family, they had meant to live in Israel, but life did not work out that way, and Geneva was now their home

Once again, the mourning period was shortened because of the Passover holiday.

That was also the year the company bought Horowitz-Margereten.

"But they're going to keep the name separate," Jack told his sister over the phone. She had stayed in the United States only long enough for the shiva and the Passover holiday, and was back with her family in Switzerland. As a shareholder, Jack kept up-to-date on company news; his sister, who lived overseas, was more detached.

Laura gave a short laugh. "At least nobody will be able to tease us any more with the old "So you're from the Manischewitz family? I have a friend at Horowitz-Margereten." Laura had suffered a lot from teasing as a kid. Having a famous name was never easy, just as her Aunt Judy used to say. Laura had been glad to exchange it for her husband's more ordinary name.

"Ho ho," said Jack. "By the way, they say that Horowitz-Margereten uses a different recipe. I say fiddlesticks. How different can a matzo be?" Jack had inherited some of his father's skepticism.

"Oh, there you're wrong, I know better," said his sister, not ashamed to flaunt her foreign experience before her brother. "In Geneva we can't get Manischewitz, so I've tasted them all. Matzo from Alsace is light and crispy, melts in your mouth. Israeli matzo is much heavier and stays in your stomach. And besides that—"

"Okay, okay," said Jack. "This is an international call."

* * *

Passover, 1990, in Geneva, Switzerland.

"If everything's ready for the Seder," says Yossi to his wife, "you've got time for some phone calls before the guests arrive. Start with Israel," he adds, "because it's already getting late there." And so the first call is to Elaine, in Israel.

"Happy holiday, Elaine" says Laura, "to all the family there." Elaine, who has no children of her own, has closed up her Haifa apartment for the holiday. She will be celebrating a Yemenite Seder with her husband, Yehiel, in his mother's home, surrounded by some of her fifty nieces and nephews, members of Yehiel's warm and loving family. As she does not need to prepare a meal, she has time to talk.

"So it looks like the company is going to be sold," says Elaine. This completes the cycle: the news has traveled around the world. "My father said it isn't final yet. (It would not be final until the following January.)

Laura asks who the buyer is, and listens to a few other details, but without great interest. "Well, you know," she says, "it's not as if we were working there."

"True," says her cousin. "I wonder how it would have been, if girls had been considered possible heirs to the company?"

"Well, I for one wouldn't have wanted to work in the company," says Laura. "My father always made it sound like there was so much pressure."

"My father, too."

Both Laura and Elaine are librarians. Elaine's job brings her in daily contact with Israeli children from many backgrounds, all of them learning day by day to read in Hebrew. She loves her job. Laura works in an international library connected to the United Nations, a fascinating world to work in.

"I wouldn't have liked being a businesswoman anyhow, I guess," she admits. "Even though I've always told my daughters that a woman can do anything a man can do. So now Sharona's studying chemistry. She already tells me she wants to work with polymers. Like, what are polymers?"

"It's the end of an era," says Elaine.

"Right."

"Well—*Pesach same'ach* to your lovely family."

"Happy holiday to you, too. And to Yehiel and all the family."

The next call is to Helen, at her home in New Jersey.

"Happy holiday, Mom."

"How lovely to hear your voice. Happy holiday."

"Mom, what do you think about the company being sold?"

"There's not much to be said." Helen has never gone in for sentimentality. "It will be for a fair price. It was getting hard for me to attend those board meetings anyway." She has been filling Howard's place on the board ever since his death. "Plus, it's not as if your brother ever worked for the company."

Hey, thinks Laura, *how come only my brother comes into consideration?* But it is too late, by about thirty years, to bring this up with her mom.

"Jack is here, let me pass him to you."

"Happy holiday, Jack. How's your work going?"

Jack is a civil servant, responsible for grants management at the National Institute on Drug Abuse. "Pretty good," he says.

"Well, hi to Jody and her folks." Jack and his wife have no children.

"Well," he echoes, "happy holiday to you and Yossi and the girls."

The last call is to Judy. She lives alone now in her New York apartment. Her children are dispersed; Elaine lives in Israel, her second daughter, Rubye (now Rivka), lives in Scranton with two of her children, and her youngest daughter, Edey, and her children live in West Virginia. Luckily Judy's sisters still live in New York and she would be celebrating the holiday with them.

"Happy holiday, Aunt Judy."

"Happy holiday to you and Yossi and the girls."

"I just spoke to Elaine." "Me too."

"What do you think about the sale of the company?"

Maybe I shouldn't have asked, Laura thinks, as soon as the words are out. Because it will not be a quick answer. Judy has been a Manischewitz her whole life. She has been the family historian and a very family-oriented person. Plus her life has been filled with all kinds of Jewish activities.

And she loves to chat.

"Well, you know," she begins, "in one way it's the end of an era. But in another way it isn't. Each person has played his role in his generation, and each time something of his work remains afterwards. The future builds on the past. The Manischewitz Company is a part of American Jewish culture, and that will continue. I expect the commitment to Israel will go on too."

"I guess so." Laura had not given it much thought.

"In the same way that your great-grandfather Behr built up the company so strongly that his five sons, each so different, couldn't have broken it down if they wanted to. They could coast on his legacy for years." She warms to the subject. "The next generation, my father and my uncles were so different from one another. Jake had Behr's love for his work, but not his religious beliefs. My father, Hirsh, had the religious beliefs, but he hadn't really learned to work for a living. And after that generation died, the men in my generation were caught in the middle."

"Uh huh." This seems like a good point to stop. There are sticky issues here, about the men in the next generation; Judy and Bernard were separated in 1972.

"Anyway, I like your idea that the legacy will go on. Happy holiday, Aunt Judy."

"Happy holiday, Laura dear. My best to your lovely family."

When the calls are over, Laura turns her attention back to the Seder table. With a practiced eye, she makes sure that nothing is missing. The candles are ready for lighting, the place settings are ready, and in the center, a silver Seder plate is set with all the items called for by tradition, some still wrapped in foil, till the guests arrive. Salt water bowls are ready with little heaps of salt, thirsting for water, which one of her daughters will add at the last minute. The three matzos for the ceremony are placed on the table in the traditional pile, under an embroidered cloth. The bottom matzo is called the Afikomen. It is the last thing to be eaten at the end of the traditional meal ; without it the ceremony cannot be completed. Which is why the long-standing tradition evolved: the father hides it, the children steal it, and they return it for a ransom. Candy, money, or larger booty: each family has its custom.

Laura turns to her husband.

"Yossi? Will you be hiding the Afikomen this year? The girls are too old to hunt for it anymore in order to win a ransom." There are a few guests expected, but no children. Sharona, home from college for the holiday, is in the bedroom with her younger sister, Eleanor, catching up on news from the high school.

"I guess not. You'll have to wait for the next generation."

Laura's face softens. But her husband, who misses nothing, shakes his head. "Don't hold your breath. This generation has what you always wished for, equality. These girls will be studying for years, and having careers too."

"Then we'll just have to wait."

"And take what life brings." In the background, the doorbell is ringing. He pats his wife's shoulder.

"Meanwhile," he says, "let's get this Seder on the road."

Sources

This book has been based largely on that most precious of sources, the oral history provided to me by family members, most of them no longer living. I filled in the gaps with my own research in libraries and archives. I traveled to Klaipeda (formerly Memel), Telsiai (Telz) and Salantai (Salant) in Lithuania to see the traces of their life before emigrating, and encountered members of the remaining Lithuanian Jewish community. I visited each of the places in Cincinnati that belong to the family's 80-year history in that city and met with people who have memories of those days. From this combination of research and family lore I have pieced together a fiction that I believe has the essence of reality as the characters themselves must have lived it. It is my hope that they would recognize themselves on these pages.

The following unpublished sources were particularly valuable:

Dov Behr Manischewitz – correspondence with his father in Lithuania and later, with his son Hirsh in Jerusalem (copies held at the American Jewish Archives, Cincinnati) (1887-1904)

Jacob U. Manischewitz and Pearl Quitman Manischewitz – letters (1909-1932)

Esther Judith Manischewitz – "Outline for a History of the Manischewitz family" and "Significant Dates in my Life"

Howard Manischewitz – diary in the form of a lifelong correspondence with his uncle, Jesse Quitman, 1922-1963

For related historical information, the following published sources are available:

About us / History, on the Internet at www.manischewitz.com
The American Israelite (weekly), Cincinnati, various years.
Mendels, Pamela, **The Modern Method of Making Matza**. In *Jewish Monthly*, April 1986, pp. 18-24.
Nathan, Joan, **Jewish Cooking in America**, expanded edition, Knopf, 1998.
Sarna, Jonathan, **How Matzah Became Square: Manischewitz and the Development of Machine-Made Matzah in the United States**. Touro College. 2005.
Sarna, Jonathan, **Manischewitz matzah and the rabbis of the Holy Land, a study in the interrelationship of business, charity and faith**. In *Gesher: Journal of Jewish Affairs*, 2001.
Sarna, Jonathan, with Nancy H. Klein, **The Jews of Cincinnati**, Hebrew Union College – Jewish Institute of Religion, 1989.
Sefer Telz / Telsiai Book, a memorial to the Jewish community of Telz (in Hebrew and Yiddish). Published by the Association of Telz Emigrants in Israel, Tel-Aviv, 1984.
The B. Manischewitz Company, **Annual report for the fiscal year ended July 31...**(various years).